GRAND RAPIDS GRASSROOTS: AN ANTHOLOGY

Edited by Ashley E. Nickels and Dani Vilella

First edition 2017
ISBN: 978-0-9980188-2-9

Belt Publishing
1667 E. 40th Street #1G1
Cleveland, Ohio 44120
www.beltmag.com

Book design by David Wilson

Similar Titles From Belt Publishing

Rust Belt Chicago: An Anthology
Right Here, Right Now: The Buffalo Anthology
The Akron Anthology
Happy Anyway: The Flint Anthology
Car Bombs To Cookie Tables: The Youngstown Anthology
The Pittsburgh Anthology
A Detroit Anthology
The Cincinnati Anthology
Rust Belt Chic: The Cleveland Anthology

TABLE OF CONTENTS

A Journey to Activism...

Bottom-Up, Top-Down...

Contributors |
Acknowledgments |

Our Act of Activism

by Ashley E. Nickels and Dani Vilella

This book is an extension of our friendship; an extension of our ongoing work...

To start, we are longtime friends—since third grade. We have known each other for decades. In fact, our first collaborative activist effort was in sixth grade. Together with our peers, we organized a petition to overturn a decision made by our school's principal. We succeeded. Long before we knew the words activism, organizing, or advocacy, we were working together to make change.

The first time we both boarded a plane we were not headed to Cancun for spring break, it was to Washington, D.C., for "CloseUp," a nationally recognized program that teaches democracy and civic engagement to high school students in the nation's capital.

In college, we travelled together again, this time to Nicaragua to study poverty and social justice issues on an international scale. In our twenties, when we decided to take a vacation together, we traveled to Guatemala to work with orphans and victims of domestic violence.

Back in our native city, our activism continued. We sat on the board for the local chapter of the National Organization for Women (NOW-GR). Through NOW-GR, we created an awards/community outreach event called "Then & NOW." We collaborated with other community groups to organize protests, demonstrations, and community events. We helped the organizers of Grand Rapids's first "SlutWalk;" we marched with Planned Parenthood and in the Grand Rapids Pride Parade; we supported women candidates for elected office.

Our activism drives our friendship as much as our friendship drives our activism. We understand that the opportunities that we were offered and took hold of reflect our privilege—white, middle-class, and college educated. We sought these experiences not to "save the world," but to learn firsthand what we had heard about in our classrooms. And we want to be clear, we don't only get together to undertake large-scale activist projects. You can often find us, our third beer in hand, playing euchre or dancing to nineties music. We have had a little fun along the way, too.

Each of these experiences was one more stepping stone in the paths that put us where we are today. Ashley is a professor of political science at Kent State University, teaching the next generation of students about urban politics, community organizing, and nonprofit advocacy, and focusing, most recently, on her research on the politics of municipal takeover in Flint, Michigan. Dani is the Advocacy and Field Manager for Planned Parenthood of Michigan, training activists, encouraging civic engagement, fighting for social justice, and teaching people about politics.

This book is the next step in our activist journey.

Editing this anthology is, for us, an act of activism, in and of itself. The process for creating this book, too, was an homage to grassroots action. From crowdfunding the book, gaining support from 121 funders, to recruiting and working with the thirty-five authors in this volume, this book has been built from the ground up.

While the concept of "grassroots" means more than just activism, the task of reaching out to the community, gathering the stories of individuals, attempting to ensure a diversity of voices, and curating this collection of snapshots of the city we know and love is yet another strategy that we are using to create conversation and change in our community.

We both grew up in Grand Rapids, went to Grand Rapids Public Schools together, and, after college, both chose Grand Rapids as the place to start our families and careers. We bought our first houses, had kids, and started our respective careers here. Ashley moved away six years ago to pursue her Ph.D. in New Jersey and has since settled in Cleveland, Ohio, but Grand Rapids is still home.

We did not want to write a book about Grand Rapids's grassroots community. We wanted to provide a platform for others to share their stories—stories about residents everyday lives and the work taking place here.

Needless to say, Grand Rapids has been a major part of our lives.

We did not know what this book would look like in the end. We reached out as far and wide and as deep as possible, hoping to draw diverse voices, perspectives, and stories. We have been surprised and humbled at the number of contributors that have put time and effort into the telling of their stories, praising and critiquing their own city and baring their vulnerabilities in the process.

While we are happy with how the book turned out, it was rough at times. As with any activist endeavor, we faced multiple challenges—time crunches, human nature, fear, and network limitations, to name a few.

Some people were too busy. Or they didn't identify as writers and felt intimidated by the prospect of putting virtual pen to paper. Some were confused about why we reached out to them, feeling like imposters who weren't qualified to take on the mantle of activist/organizer/storyteller, often asking, "What have I ever done?" or saying, "I don't even know what I would write about." For many, it was too personal of a request and people were uncomfortable writing about themselves and taking ownership of their work in the community. These are all understandable human responses to being asked to contribute to a book.

More disturbingly, however, we often encountered people who wanted to write about exciting, controversial topics critiquing "the system," who, when faced with the actual task of putting their thoughts on paper, realized that it could jeopardize their livelihoods or funding for their current projects, or burn bridges with people in power that they needed to maintain. This problem hits at the very reason that this book needs to exist. Grand Rapids is a city too often defined and designed by the wealthy power players who hold real sway over the ability of people on the ground to do the work that needs to be done.

While we tried hard to reach out as broadly and deeply into the community as was possible, not every issue of importance is represented here, not every community is present. We recognize and acknowledge these gaps. Like all activist projects, there is room for improvement and things we would do differently if we were to do it again. Because of these issues, it is just as important to read not only the stories that are represented, but the spaces in between them. The voices that are missing are just as much a part of this tale. This book is a snapshot in time; it reflects parts of Grand Rapids today, while trying to acknowledge its complex histories.

As happens in many cities, the dominant narratives about Grand Rapids and its citizens do not often align with the lived experiences of the people on the ground.

Contrary to the common perceptions, we are not all wealthy, white, conservative philanthropists. Grand Rapids is more than Amway, ArtPrize, Medical Mile, or the DeVos and VanAndel families. Recently we have come to be known as Beer City USA. This exciting, yet dubious title, provides us with an example to show the complexity of this paradox. Don't get us wrong, we love beer, and the local breweries, but people who want to push development and tourism too often dominate the conversation, and people are being left behind, neighborhoods are being broken up, and voices are being silenced. While it has increased tourism and put dollars in the coffers of local businesses, it has also become a symbol of rampant development, gentrification, and skyrocketing housing costs disproportionately affecting the city's more marginalized citizens.

While not all of the powers-that-be have an adversarial relationship with those who identify with the grassroots, due to the historical and social context of the city, there is a significant amount of antagonism between those with money and power and the people impacted by the use of that money and power. The local power of the purse is located in the hands of a few, who have their own agenda, and as such, the projects that they will support or fund are too often limited in scope or not responsive to the changing needs, identities, and demographics of communities within Grand Rapids.

This tension between development, growth, and progress, and those with the money and power to back it, versus the individuals, organizations, and communities that are creatively, innovatively, and doggedly attempting to make the city livable for everyone else, sits at the heart of many of the pieces in this book. It was our intent to provide a platform for people to tell the world about grassroots Grand Rapids—those people, groups, and organizations doing the often-hidden (or marginalized) work of community organizing, political and civic mobilization, and neighborhood building. When communities are marginalized, those voices are left out of important decision-making processes. Their interests are not heard; their expertise is not valued. We are more than rapid economic development. We are more than our industries. We are more than the big names plastered on the side of buildings. As Grand Rapids continues to grow and thrive, we need to bring the voices of the most marginalized to the center.

This is our small contribution to that process, our act of defiance.

Of the People

...where we hear stories of life in Grand Rapids

Searching this City's Thrift Stores for Mirrors

by Z.G. Tomaszewski

> *I rejected*
> *the comforts I had contrived for myself; I exchanged them*
> *for a rain of small faces on the abandoned street.*
>
> *– Donald Hall, The One Day*

Looking along each aisle for any sharp angle of light,
I walk past discarded hats and exhumed outfits,
past pots and pans and "Jesus Loves You" and "God
As Your Witness" signs, until finally a spark steps out
from that darkness and there's one wavy sheet of
glass like a lake surface petrified and my figure
stenciled and groovy like a drawing from the sixties in
a wanderer's notebook—a sketch in one of Hesse's
journals: like the Alps looming behind him, there's
a largeness that follows me. To each of us our luggage.
With every glance I let go, one aisle and another
gone. Remembered mountains now flattening
with distance. Clouds pulled apart by a single
thread that I take and tie around my waist, a safe rope
of light to descend by. I climb into the basement of
the Salvation Army, fluorescent dance of bulbs
flicking Morse code, and fight my way through old
shoes, march past candleholders holding no candles,
come upon a frame and my figure, again, lit right there
in the middle of it. Then the doorbell blinks and
light becomes sound as a past self exits, or enters.

This piece was previously published in Blackbird.

Down on Wealthy Street

by Z.G. Tomaszewski

When I was young and hungry,
far from home, I found a box and
folded inside.

Wrinkled skin like cardboard.

Night gave insulation
from cold eyes.

What is the basis of your salvation?

The man at the off ramp
is a billboard for hunger.
He holds a sign.
Hopeless, you think.

I laugh nervously when a friend tells me
how awkwardly he reacts
when he drives by a bum,
but has to stop for a red light.

I, too, am guilty.

The light turns green, I take off slowly.
I remember what feeds me.
It's part of the burden.

These two poems roam through the wilderness of self in city, inhabiting the restlessness of James Wright's Shall We Gather at the River, discovering, in one's longing, that there is always double, or as Robert Frost remarked, inner and outer weather. I think both poets speak to the climate of the have-nots and the search for enough ground to call one's own. The poems here serve a side of Grand Rapids seen from the lens of a native who has left and returned, repeatedly. We all wish to belong, somehow, somewhere, and these pieces inspect and reflect such personal orientations in the city.

This piece was previously published in the 3228 *Review.*

My Grand Rapids

by Dia Penning

My Grand Rapids was a collision of the Pentecostal and Christian Reformed churches, Aquinas College, the YWCA, City High, and the public library. My Grand Rapids was summer festivals and winter food drives, East Grand Rapids and East Town, public and private, and rich and poor. My Grand Rapids was for being righteous, doing good, and not asking too many questions. My Grand Rapids was and is a city of duality, a city where you can live multiple experiences at once, and yet still feel invisible.

I was born in 1974 to a white mother and a Black father. We lived off Eastern Avenue behind a big church. Our windows didn't seal well, we had mice and roaches. My mother often was referred to as being "one of those girls." We listened to Marvin Gaye and Fleetwood Mac and swam in the river. I didn't know that people stared at me because I was usually one of the only black faces in a sea of white. I knew I was different but I didn't grasp the depth of that difference until well into my twenties. My mother taught me that I was a jewel, a precious and perfect thing that others wished they could emulate.

For a black girl with a white mom, growing up in Grand Rapids was confusing. I occupied spaces that were not for me. I endured micro aggressions, misunderstanding, hair touching, tone policing, and yet I didn't understand that these interactions were shaping me to ask why, to demand answers, and to fight for the right to ask them. At the time, I realized that the world I was experiencing and the one that I was being told existed were two very different worlds.

My head was filled with questions. In church, I was asked to leave my Sunday school classes because my hand was constantly in the air. I was told that we accepted on faith, that things were the way they were for a reason. That I didn't have to know why. I couldn't fathom that my family, the people I played with, and the churches I attended experienced a different reality.

I didn't understand. I wanted to know why.

I listened to sermons extolling the virtues of selfless service and cooperation. I heard in those same spaces assumptions about people who looked like me and the exclamations of the necessity of saving them from themselves—their ignorance and childlikeness being a marker of their need for saving. It was infinitely confusing, and while I participated in youth groups, food drives, walk-a-thons and all-night dance fundraisers, I felt separate. Not only because of my race, or my parents' relationship, but because I wanted to understand. As long as I didn't ask questions, I would fit; because I was invisible, my difference would lay only on my skin. We could all pretend that it wasn't really that big of a deal. I had to choose between being included but invisible or being an outsider and understanding more about the world around me.

I have never been one who exists much in the past. The things that are happening to me right now—teaching, parenting, activism, writing, making art, driving car pool, napping between these—take much more energy and attention, so when I received an email from a fellow City High School graduate asking me about a government class project from 1991, I had a hard time placing it. My remembered experience of high school was, as for many, a blur of all night studying, car trips to Chicago, snarky one-liners to patient teachers, and gratitude that I had managed to become an adult in spite of the self-loathing and confusion. The email was simple, asking if I remembered a project about the jury selection process.

I did not.

So, let me be clear, though I struggled with my own identity and confusion growing up, I was not the most reflective of children. I was and am a big personality and I asked a lot of questions, due to my curiosity and the outside pressure to not be curious. I don't recall being particularly justice-oriented. I just wanted to know why intent and impact didn't match up. I was very, um, shall we say, linear in my thought. If there are A and B, then the logical conclusion is C. If you say that you are doing something to better humanity and you put in that time, your internal landscape must be one of altruism…right?

My former schoolmate explained to me that the project was looking at the pool of jury candidates for trial cases and that we were examining how juries were created. I had asked a question about the process. In my seventeen-year-old mind, I could not imagine that in a city like Grand Rapids, the pool of selectable candidates would not reflect the actual population. To me, it just didn't fit my logic model. So I asked why, as I frequently did. This question sent my government teacher on a ten-year quest with successive groups of students to examine the process and to interrogate the systems that put it into place, to rail against the unfairness of it all. He took that all the way to the U.S. Supreme Court. For me, it was just a question.

My life has been a series of questions, some in response to inequity, some in response to being told not to ask questions. My life, that became one of activism—running a consulting company that works with universities, tech companies, artists, and governments to make structural and lasting change, raising a black boy in Oakland, California, and being an out lesbian in the time of culture wars—has been based on a series of questions.

When you call my mom "one of those girls," what does that mean?

Why do you say one thing and do another?

What can I do to make the world reflect the world that I was told existed?

If you don't serve those with less, how can you consider yourself a Christian?

Why would we pass laws that create a system of oppression for an entire group of people based on race, gender, ability, or sexuality?

I asked a lot of questions. I was told not to a lot, always, constantly. I got in trouble for asking questions, kicked out of classrooms, sent to the principal's office, grounded. Asking questions makes you visible. It makes you loud. For someone like me, who lived in two different worlds (on the margins of both) and who was largely invisible, I wanted to be heard. I wanted to be seen.

If people saw me, maybe they would see that separations were arbitrary. Maybe we could live in the world that we all claimed we were working toward. As I grew and incorporated more information into my understanding of the world, I've asked more questions.

Why should some mothers have to worry more than other mothers about the safety of their children?

Why do you hate people because of who they marry?

Why can't we all trust the police in the same way?

Why are Black people, Latino people, Asian people kept separate?

Why are poor people poor and why does it cost more for them?

What is the point of money? Where is it going and why?

Who is making these decisions?

It was my experience of Grand Rapids that molded this part of me, the part that fueled the questions and at the same time wanted to silence them. Living at the margins of two worlds, I had to be duplicitous, emotionally attuned. I witnessed that the intent of one community often had an opposite impact; I wanted to know why. I wanted to know why no one talked, why we didn't work in collaboration with one another. I wanted to know why we were closed to questions that would actually create change and why no one listened to people whose experience could help answer them.

So now, decades later, I live in Oakland, California. My Oakland is not that different from my Grand Rapids. It has many, if not more, of the same problems. I ask the same questions. I support people in thinking things through for themselves, sharing information and history and impact that so many of my family members and friends never had access to. I do it all to answer my own questions—my questions of who I am, how I hold value in the world, and how that value can support the development of a more thoughtful and intentional space for us all.

Grand Rapids taught me duality. My activism is to develop wholeness and at the same time to be able to hold paradox.

Zen and the Art of Moped Negligence
by Troy Reimink

Halfway back to Grand Rapids in a warm downpour, my Puch's
engine hiccupped, then sputtered and wheezed its last breath of
the summer. We had split from the rest of the rally pack while
everyone else set up camp under a park pavilion to wait out the
storm and extend their communal whiskey bender. I was in a
surf punk band called the Postures with Cedric, who was riding alongside me, and we had to play a show that night at a tiny
sports bar in the city's then-desolate northwest quadrant that
had no business booking live music. I hastily refilled my gas
tank before the trip home, but gave it an oil mix that was too
rich for the engine to handle, and the moped crapped out on me
for the second time that day.

Even in clear weather, on a smooth and flat road, I could barely top twenty-five miles per hour. Unlike most riders, I had never bothered to upgrade my moped's stock parts, a fact I clung
to pridefully in the same annoying manner of people who brag
about not having tattoos. The Michigan Vehicle Code, as of 2015,
defines a moped as a two- or three-wheeled motorized bike with
an engine up to 100 cubic centimeters that does not exceed thirty
miles per hour and does not have a gearshift. The law fails to account for a signature characteristic of the moped lifestyle, which
is that almost everyone takes a vintage frame or chassis and
builds it out with engine and exhaust enhancements that facilitate ridiculously unsafe speeds. My bike was the slowest in that
year's Ghost Ride rally—this was 2007, so that would have been
the second annual—but it did fit the technical definition, which
meant that after I left, the rally still contained about 100 bikes,
but, legally speaking, almost zero actual mopeds.

Cedric's Honda Passport was more of a scooter. Under pen-
alty of severe ridicule, the words "moped" and "scooter" are not
to be used interchangeably. The Wikipedia page for "moped" is
emphatic on this point, explaining in its opening paragraph how
calling a scooter a moped is—*clears throat—"quite erroneous."*

The typical scooter has a greater engine displacement, moves faster, has a foot platform and, well, looks like a scooter. But the subcultures are hospitable to each other's members, perhaps in solidarity against the outside perception that all of us are too chicken-livered to buy real motorcycles.

If an ordinary person were to close their eyes and hear the word "moped," my 1977 Puch Maxi is close to the image it would conjure. In the 2000s, old step-through Puch bikes in the Maxi family—those with in-frame gas tanks rather than the top-tankers that more closely resemble dirt bikes—appeared in movies like *Spider-Man 2* and *Little Miss Sunshine* as narrative shorthand for a vague sort of Wes Anderson-like hipsterdom. There is a magnetism to the Maxi that is hard to quantify but also hard to deny, something both retro-chic and future-dystopian about the granny-bicycle shape of its body, its bulbous headlight, and the pedals that protrude from the frame like little T. Rex arms.

The pedals, of course, are the real distinction between a moped and a scooter—and for that matter, a motorcycle, a pickup truck, a golf cart or a horse. "Moped" derives from the combination of motor and pedals; starting the latter requires rotation of the former. The intention is for a moped to function as both a motorized bike and, after an inevitable breakdown, a normal bike. Except a person pedaling a moped with a stalled engine is a pitiful sight, and a metaphor widely applicable to the human experience.

It certainly felt that way while I plodded along, demoralized a little more with the spray of each passing vehicle. It was the second time my moped died that day. Cedric was idling a short distance ahead, leading the way to the home of a cousin he said lived nearby. Two miles of grunting, cursing, and life-decision-questioning later, we found his house, toweled off, and pleaded for a ride to Grand Rapids and a place in the garage to stash my bike until we could recover it with the band van.

"Sure," he said. Then, after a pause: "Why don't you guys just get motorcycles?"

***

The grassroots vintage moped community that exists and thrives throughout the United States originated in West Michigan. It is one of our region's great contributions to world culture, along with office furniture, craft beer, and "The Freshmen." In 1997, three moped enthusiasts at Western Michigan University in Kalamazoo, fifty miles south of Grand Rapids, formed a group called the Decepticons. Through online networking and annual rallies that drew hundreds of riders from across the country, a national movement began to coalesce. By the turn of the century, the Decepticons had become the ground-zero fleet of the nationwide Moped Army. In 2003, one of the founders opened 1977 Mopeds, a retail outlet, warehouse, repair shop, and spiritual mecca that still operates today. The Army now boasts about twenty chapters, including two others in Michigan—Detroit's Motor City Riot and Grand Rapids's Ghost Riders, who received official status in 2004 and have remained a strong presence ever since.

The Ghost Ride rally happens in and around Grand Rapids in mid-to-late August as a late-summer complement to the corresponding event in Kalamazoo over Memorial Day weekend. Each summer there are at least a dozen rallies around the country—from Dayton to Austin, Philadelphia to Omaha, Chicago to Toledo—that will draw chapter representatives from far and wide. Alongside the official Army branches, there are also hundreds of un- or quasi-affiliated groups and gangs that exist at the periphery, all of whom are welcome to participate. The organization prides itself on eschewing all intra-cultural drama—a noble goal that it almost achieves, and which I would inadvertently violate.

I had bought my Maxi on a whim at the beginning of summer 2007. I was working at Vertigo Music, the popular Grand Rapids record store, which for a few years headquartered the local moped scene while its owner, Herm Baker, refurbished and resold vintage bikes. During one of my regular Monday night shifts, someone dropped off a moped in good condition whose intended purchaser had backed out. Herm saw me eyeing the bike and delivered a cautious sales pitch, explaining the advantages to moped ownership—inexpensiveness, fuel-efficiency, instant access to a social circle known for partying at Andrew W. K. levels of intensity—as well as the downsides.

"You're going to spend the entire summer smelling like gasoline and covered in grease. So don't plan on dating very much," he said (I'm paraphrasing), inspecting the Puch and performing various screw-tightenings and other confounding maintenance rituals. "Also, don't listen to people who talk about the green benefits of these machines. You have to combine the gas with two-stroke engine oil, so it's like riding a lawnmower around the city. It's actually much worse for the environment!"

He held up a hand for a high-five, which I obliged. I agreed to take the bike home in exchange for a down payment and several months of counter duty. Working every Monday, though, meant I probably would not become part of the Ghost Riders, who always met that night at Founders Brewing Co. for their weekly group rides. I already had a few friends with mopeds who were similarly schedule-conflicted and unaffiliated, so we formed our own loose organization, which we would call—*clears throat again—the Moped Navy.

Our bylaws were as follows:

- Official gatherings shall not be referred to as meetings, but as "drinkings." A drinking shall consist of a group ride (or "sail") or literally just drinking.

- All riders ("sailors") shall wear nautical attire during Navy sailings/drinkings.

- At the beginning of each drinking, the leader ("captain") of the previous sail shall be deposed by mutiny and ceremoniously replaced. Upon assuming authority, each new captain shall make a decree to be observed during that day's sailing/drinking.

- No less often than once per month in the summer, the Navy shall sail en masse to the nearest Red Lobster and get thrown out.

- Once every summer, the Navy shall organize a Fleet Week, to consist of group sailings/drinkings, a Captain's Cotillion ball, a Parade of Ships (mopeds decorated as floats) and an informative health fair for scurvy-related ailments.

The group—me, Cedric, Brooke, Lydia, Tedros, and various other comers and goers in response to Facebook postings—spent the summer discussing these ideas at the Meanwhile Bar and implementing zero of them. Still, as the Ghost Ride approached, our insurgent organization had ruffled some feathers within the official Moped Army branch, who interpreted the name Moped Navy as disrespectful (rather than a sincere acknowledgement of inferiority). Phil, our Army liaison, strongly suggested that we minimize the Navy's visible presence during rally weekend. Which, fair enough: we were going to be participating in rides and parties they organized and in all likelihood consuming a lot of their Pabst Blue Ribbon. Out of deference, I scrubbed off the anchor I had markered onto my arm.

The rally schedule called for long daytime rides on Saturday and Sunday, plus a late night trek through Greenwood Cemetery off Leonard Street. I would only make one ride before my forced seasonal retirement; this was the same day as the rainstorm. The first leg of the trip was equally blunderous, even though it did begin promisingly. We met early Saturday at Sixth Street Bridge Park for the big kickoff, limiting our Navy regalia to the matching Sperry Topsiders we'd all taken to wearing. Various scattered factions gathered under their respective flags. A collective whoop pierced the morning air, and engines revved in a demonic chorus, trebly and insect-like. (The national Moped Army's slogan, "Swarm and Destroy," embraces this.)

The sound of a single moped is almost mournful, like guitar feedback that trails off at the end of a song. A rally in full force is apocalyptic. You might hear a far-off whine while watering your lawn some summer night and not give it a moment's thought. But maybe the noise, the endless long-E buzzsaw, doesn't fade into the sky. Maybe one time, it keeps getting louder, and the mosquito finds your ear canal and brings several hundred of its friends. You're standing dumbfounded in the driveway, a flaccid hose spilling water wastefully down the pavement and on to your subdivision's street as one rider goes by, then another, then a small cluster, then the massive main group, paying you the scarcest attention, an unknowable story behind each bike, each helmet sticker, each tattoo.

The pack left Sixth Street Bridge Park and made its way down Monroe Avenue, through downtown and on to Market Avenue. The faster riders performed herding duty, pulling ahead to block each intersection and allowing the whole group to pass through together, traffic signals notwithstanding. We ended up on Market Avenue, then the smooth, tree-lined Indian Mounds Trail along the Grand River, then caught Wilson Avenue and stopped at a gas station before heading north. As soon as we got back on the road, my drive chain dislodged from the rear wheel sprocket and I ground to an abrupt halt. I was near the back of the group, and chains are a more complicated fix than they might seem, so I was unable to get it back on in time to catch up. On each big rally ride, a few members volunteer to pilot a support vehicle for broken-down mopeds. The rented U-Haul tailed the pack and found me, hands hopelessly coated in chain grease, failing to get the links onto the teeth, loving life. Promising help once the group made it to the park, the guys lifted my bike into the back of the truck. Since there was no room in the cab, I was stuck back there as well, in a pitch-black unventilated swelter where the only place to sit was atop stacks of product from that year's rally sponsor, Four Loko, an alcoholic energy drink that was later banned in Michigan. By the time we reached the park, I had downed three piping-hot, fetid cans.

Like any club, moped culture is full of people who often have little in common besides the one thing that draws them together. But one trait almost everyone shares is a generosity with time, tools, and information. Everything on a moped will break, but rarely in a way that nobody else has experienced, and there's no better place for a breakdown than amidst the collective knowledge base of a rally. When the support truck reached the park and the door slid open, a half-dozen riders had gathered around to see how they could assist whomever was inside, no matter what city or gang they represented, if any—or maybe they were just thirsty for some of that sweet Four Loko. Either way, I got my chain fixed, found Cedric, and prepared to depart as the late-afternoon clouds darkened.

I would learn in subsequent summers—after innumerable fouled spark plugs, clogged pilot jets, leaky carburetors and flat tires—that you can repair a moped all you want, but you'll never really have it fixed. You are always between one equipment failure and the next.

Again with the metaphors.

***

In 2005, the Kalamazoo artist and writer Paul Sizer published a graphic novel called Moped Army, which he based partly on the moped culture in his hometown. It's a dystopian story set 250 years in the future, when cities are built upward on the wreckage of crumbled infrastructure, and the wealthy live literally in the sky. A girl from the upper class, unsatisfied with her comfortable life, is drawn to the underground, where gangs of moped riders—tattooed, bearded, and be-flannelled—fight for survival among the ruins. It's science fiction, but it's hard not to recognize the world as an exaggerated version of what the streets look like from the seat of a moped. The city that reveals itself isn't a community that has a place for you, but an indifferent landscape where just to exist feels like getting away with something, where you're always riding on paths not meant for you.

There is a grain of literal truth to this. Mopeds occupy a gray space on the roads and in the law. Parking one, for example, can be Kafkaesque experience; I once got ticketed for chaining mine to a bike rack on city property, and learned local ordinance forbids parking any vehicle with a motor on a sidewalk. But occupying a whole metered spot, as would a motorcycle, doesn't make any sense. When I asked where I could legally put my moped, a representative with the Grand Rapids parking department said there was one parking ramp downtown that had a designated scooter zone, and that was my only option. (I resisted the opportunity to explain how erroneous it is to call a moped a scooter and vice versa. To recap: quite!) Moped riders also are required to behave, when possible, like bicyclists, hugging the right side of the road, using hand signals for turns, riding no more than two side-by-side, etc. Mopeds are fast enough to move at the speed of traffic on many city streets, but not so fast that cars won't pass on the left at the first opportunity, which can make riding a moped extremely dangerous. There is an ambiguity to the relationship between cars and mopeds that cyclists—for all the unique dangers they face—do not have to contend with.

But something else about the grim world of Moped Army rings even truer than the lifestyle's intrinsic outsider status, or the society of misfits Sizer vividly depicts. Riding through Grand Rapids, you can watch a different sort of dystopia take shape in real time. It's no exaggeration to say this is a different city in 2017 than it was ten years ago when I started riding mopeds here. A dizzying development boom has accompanied Grand Rapids's self-branding as "Beer City USA." The dive bars we'd visit during our Navy sailings, if they still stand at all, now exist in the shadows of massive mixed-use projects with luxury condos, artisanal brewpubs, and box-like restaurants. The city's gentrification is entwined with a multifaceted housing crisis.

Neighborhoods as diffuse as Eastown, Creston Heights, Belknap, Midtown, Heartside, Westside Connection, and East Hills are filling with disconcertingly similar housing developments whose units—mostly with rents that are inaccessible to working-class residents—disappear faster than developers can build them. At one point in 2015, Grand Rapids had the lowest rental availability rate in the United States. That's alarming, since nearly half of all foreclosed homes sold in Grand Rapids since the 2008 housing crash were purchased by investors as rental properties, according to a Michigan Radio report. List after list of "hot" housing markets (Trulia, Realtor.com, Forbes) puts Grand Rapids at or near the top. Houses are snatched the day they appear on the market, usually for thousands more than their asking price. City leaders no longer pretend displacement isn't occurring.

What does a community where this is happening look like in twenty years? Will once-distinct neighborhoods vanish into a blur of boutique commerce and upscale housing? As the city increasingly becomes a playground for the privileged, where will meaningful culture originate? Will the far-off whine of fifty cc engines vanish into the suburbs?

***

My moped repair skills never progressed beyond the embarrassingly rudimentary. I might be able to reassemble a carburetor, but otherwise I remain at the mercy of others. But as long as I've remembered to drain the gas before winter, the Maxi has started up on the first attempt each year. I remain a dedicated non-practitioner of the art of moped maintenance. The bike has long since paid for itself in saved gas dollars, and my growing thirty-something paranoia toward avoidable injuries means I'll probably abandon the hobby once the machine stops cooperating. Let's call it an experiment in entropy.

I can tell if it's going to be a good summer as soon as I try the Fountain Street hill. It's not the worst incline on that side of Grand Rapids. That would be Michigan Street starting at Monroe, which connects downtown to the Medical Mile and is a nightmare on any two-wheeled vehicle. Fulton is not much better. People riding eastward on bicycles know it's worth going a few blocks south to take Cherry or Wealthy. Fountain is somewhere in the middle—both attainable and enough of a challenge to feel edified if you make it on the first attempt.

With luck, the light at Ransom Avenue—which cuts the hill in half at the Grand Rapids Community College campus—will remain green. If not, you'll be starting halfway up, facing the gnarliest part of the hill and a symbolically difficult kickoff to the season. But if you make the light, your engine will hit its sweet spot right as the hill is at its steepest, and the momentum you built up after turning from Division Avenue will guide you comfortably over the top. Then, the city is your oyster. I'll cruise up Fountain past Houseman Field—the pavement is friendly and pothole-free all the way—then take Diamond Avenue to Lake Drive and head toward Eastown. I'll do a soft left on to Wealthy Street, avoiding its nightmarish cobblestones, and enter the posh neighboring city of East Grand Rapids, where the roads are immaculate. I'll go through the Gaslight Village until the street ends at Reeds Lake. From there, a trek around the water on Reeds Lake Boulevard—where you can tour past lakeside mansions on a smelly, noisy, obsolete, unwelcome machine—is one of the greatest moped afternoons ever.

These days, I mostly ride alone. I went to a few more rallies and decided they weren't my thing anymore, and maybe they never were. Even at my peak, I was at most a tertiary presence in the community. People more active in the mid- to late aughts might read this and wonder who I was. That's fine; I wasn't sure either. On a solo ride, there are few sights more heartening than a dozen kids I don't know, wearing mustaches of unclear ironic intent, riding Puchs, Yamahas, Ducatis, or Motobecanes from the oncoming direction. We'll exchange waves and nods and I'll continue on, comforted by, if not quite drawn back to, the buzz of the fading swarm.

42°57'40.5" N, 85°39' 20.59" W

by Mark Nickels

I distrust nostalgia these days.

Nostalgia is informed by the feeling that a whole era came to an end with your childhood, but the fact is that if you've lived in the last two hundred years or so, it would be hard for most humans in industrialized countries, chosen at random, to feel differently: there has been more change packed in to even the last hundred years than at any time prior, a phantasmagoria that must have my ninety-three-year-old mother, I think, reeling.

I'm talking about the qualia of life, the phenomena against which you measure the feeling of being alive.

But there is memory, which, according to those who study these things, is a little neuronal tree growing out of another neuron at each iteration; it's not a copy of an existing memory, but a new production informed by the old one somehow, altering imperceptibly each time. Imagine a billiard ball striking another, but then changing color a little before it rolls to a stop.

My Grand Rapids Era was roughly one generation, 1964-1994. I don't count the first three years because I was probably most focused on the mysterious yard—or the mysterious yards—of the neighbors, with the horizontal box elders and the tarry Depression brick you could, conceivably, peel off in hot sunlight. I confused this with an illustrated Grimm's Fairy Tales I had in which Hansel and Gretel plucked candy and cake from the house of the witch. Still more I was focused on the rooms of my house, which comprised a kingdom. I borrowed the place names for each room from the back of the phone book: Jamestown, Georgetown, Ottawa. Stuffed animals had roles to play. The bed was the palace and the dresser the Houses of Parliament, the symbol of representative democracy which is now a few feet away from me, a half-century older still.

When old enough to venture further, across skywalks (now dismantled), to Lamoreaux's Drugs at Division Avenue and Thirty-sixth Street— where wax bottles with a sugary syrup in them, or candied false teeth could be purchased, and where a deer entered the store, inexplicably, through the plate glass window—I glimpsed the cradle-emptying and the grave-filling of many things, though I didn't know this. My neighborhood had parades, rather lengthy ones, or so it seemed to me, past Mark's Photo and Carlson's Florists and Fat Man's Fish Fry and Earl Robson's Department Store, with the high school band and floats. The parades seemed to stop in the early seventies, when so many things stopped, and as far as I know they haven't started again. Godwin Heights built a new high school but the neighborhood—which didn't have far to fall in the first place— began to get a bit seedy, and Division Avenue started to decline into forties-era unzoned frumpiness.

Twenty-eighth Street—where had already long begun to take first place in hosting new forms of late twentieth-century ugliness. When I was still very small, they removed the Kent County Airport across the street, leaving, for perhaps a decade only, enormous runways with copses of aspen growing in the drainage ditches, leaving impromptu ball fields and the odd mulberry tree, and hiding places. In some weathers, it was as windswept and drab as bombed-out Berlin, but in fair weather, the sky buzzed with small, gas-powered, radio-controlled airplanes that droned like the Blue Max.

At home on the television, the WOOD TV weatherman sometimes did broadcasts on the sidewalk downtown on Monroe, the snow falling in front of a chalkboard with the requisite statistics, there in front of the great family-owned department stores, Herpolsheimer's, Steketee's, and Wurzburg's, with its wood floors and brass elevator clocks. There were huge haloes around lights as in early video, as though you'd just gotten out of a chlorinated pool. I could be wrong about that. I'm not wrong about the great movie theatres, the Savoy and the Majestic, at one of which my Aunt Ardith treated me to Disney's Bluebeard's Ghost, or, much later, when I took the bus downtown myself, Allen's Books, where I bought the endless series of Bantam Hermann Hesse paperbacks that preoccupied me as an adolescent.

On the corner was Gerry Dodd at Dodd's Record Shop, a little dour, but a wizard to my eyes. I wonder what he thought about the sixteen-year-old kid buying boxed sets of symphonies? The child, fifty-six years old now, wonders at memory as a series of nested Russian dolls: the way the sixteen-year-old, with his music and the books from the Grand Rapids Public Library (Walter Kaufmann seemed to somehow have a hand in all of them, and they were way over his head), was nostalgic for places and times he had never known. Now he recalls a place and time almost as dim in the egalitarian patina of the vanished: it feels the same if it's been 100 years, or fifty.

You can't be blamed for feeling like you dreamt the entire thing: Betty Trill's Texaco Station at Michigan and College, with its requisite commercial jingle. There was the old woman in her rocking chair under the marquee of Granny's Kitchen (who was probably neither old nor a woman) and Miller's Ice Cream in Alger Heights, where mom took me if we hadn't locked horns at the beauty parlor. I guess Fruit Basket Flowerland is still there, astonishingly. The House of Flavors at Thirty-sixth and Burlingame had bubble gum ice cream. At Varsity Barbershop I waited for my Princeton while reading Casper the Friendly Ghost comics, and decided to be a barber, which now, it seems, is never going to happen. Ditto becoming Perry Como. As the great Michigander Jim Harrison once said, "We don't get to be anybody else."

And we don't get to be from anywhere else. Woodland Skating Rink and "Troglodyte" by the Jimmy Castor Bunch. CCD at St. John Vianney where I thought the "nuns from behind the Iron Curtain" I had heard of so often were rattling the iron curtains that separated hallways after being trapped there at night, and where, amazingly, someone thought we should do magazine collages about the My Lai massacre. Bruce Grant on WOOD radio on god-awful cold mornings and god-awful Anne Murray tunes. Gaslight Village in the old museum, which helped ignite a lifelong passion for "what happened on this spot?" In the summer, I rode my bike south and east of town, the rapids on the Thornapple River at Alaska Park my destination. My sister taught me to to swim at Green Lake, and I don't think I could find it now if I had to. There was John Ball Park, with its statue of a garden-variety land shark as bearded benevolent patriarch. Skunk cabbage hollows in the old, old, old land down along the river between Grand Rapids and Wyoming, a haunt for hoboes and ghosts, maybe... children's voices and the musical bark of the axe. My mother always got me sugary "orange slices" from the candy counter at Montgomery Ward. There was Catholic Central High School, and doing theatre there with the late great Judith Hilla, across from the Herkimer Hotel, which had family associations going back decades, but which had seen better times. In a February thaw it was blue and cold and snowmelt ran braided in the gutters of cobblestoned Sheldon Avenue, and I might have been in Bremen or Krakow, what with the bells, the pigeons. I don't even have room here for the eighties.

Oh, the eighties, our sister decade.

Now I live in Pelham, Massachusetts, just up the hill from Emily Dickinson's house over in Amherst. The night is loud with tree frogs and there were wood thrush before dark just as there were at dawn, a New England summer night. Next week I'll be driving back there, Grand Rapids, and expect to be astonished, as I was the last time, at a city far more deeply cosmopolitan, with better food, where many of the same problems and wonders abide. As do the hills, harder to see, and the rivers, perhaps easier. I'm dying to know how it has changed again, and fearful at the same time. As the German singer Nico says in an album released when I was six, "I vant to know, should I stay or should I go and do I have to do just one? And can I choose again if I should lose the reason?" Memory is something of a lightning storm, properly understood, not a Joseph Cornell box. And what happened to the blue and pink neon sign, Wimpy in his car in front of Wimpy's Hamburgers, next to the Jim Williams Motor Hotel? I might distrust nostalgia, but in a dream, I pay cash to a guy as old as me named Dwayne and load it into the back of my Prius. I'll clean it up and hang it on the wall back here, back east, three cities into the future. Nostalgia lives.

LA Seems Nice in the Winter

by Joel Potrykus

A somewhat famous filmmaker once told me, "You move to LA when they want you there." It was 2012; I was in Munich, touring Europe with the first feature film I'd directed. I picked brains at every party, every meeting, figuring out how to navigate this new world of film festivals and agents and distributors and investors and producers and foie gras. Mostly, I was wondering if I needed to move to LA. Move there when they want you there. Made sense.

A tiny group of friends and I had made a film called Ape. We lived in Grand Rapids, Michigan, removed from any type of entertainment industry. We weren't paying much attention to what everyone else was doing, how they were doing it, or how much it was costing them. We scraped together a few dollars from an optimistic friend. We went in naïve enough to think we could pull it off with only a camera, microphone, and a script, but confident enough with idea of making something that'd give a middle finger to the cornball fluff that surrounded us. We wanted to make an impact in Michigan. That's about it. Never talked much about the world outside our own borders.

Somehow, we pulled it off. And got lucky. Really lucky. The very first film festival we all went to was the Locarno Film Festival in Switzerland. One of the biggest film festivals in the world. We were dizzy from the Alps and sophisticated cinephiles. One thousand people at our world premiere. And we were just some dudes from Grand Rapids. I remember talking with two Canadian filmmakers who were there with a first feature as well. They'd also worked with a small, intimate crew, and like us, "stole" most of their shots (meaning they didn't get permission or permits to film in certain locations). Our films were both small and focused on one character. We had a lot in common, coming from a part of the world only a half-day drive away from each other. Talk of budget naturally comes up with first-timers. They worked with a low budget. Really low budget. $50,000. To us, that seemed like a fortune, but in the world of filmmaking, that's your catering costs. Most independent feature films run around $300,000. Ape cost $2,500. Once that number was out of the bag, the whispers started. People didn't believe it. We had no idea.

I began to get pegged as a "grassroots filmmaker." I wasn't buying it. "Grassroots" sounded like a word I'd never use. It sounded pretentious, self-important. It sounded like something a hippie would say. Too earthy a word. For a long time, I didn't see what the fuss was about, mostly because I didn't have the perspective. We all lived and worked in Grand Rapids, and didn't even work on other films. Only after talking with other filmmakers over the course of years did I realize how differently our gang goes about business.

We kept at it, returning to Locarno two years later with a film called Buzzard.

Right around then, LA came calling. I landed an LA manager who immediately asked if I was moving there. Opportunities to direct commercials, meet all the right people. A big-time talent agency was interested in signing me. Our lead actor, Joshua, picked up and moved there, finding success. He suggested I give it a shot, too. They'd take care of me out there.

LA wanted me. I had some thinking to do.

Most art happens because it's just what the artist does. They have a routine, a life, people around them always asking what they're up to and who want to hear all about what's next. There's a gentle pressure to impress them, to keep going. These are the things that make art possible. Environment. This was my theory, and I wasn't sure I could even do what I did out there. LA is full of film people asking about your permit, your insurance, whether or not you're a union production. That seemed more foreign and unappealing than the foie gras. I don't like red tape. I don't like duck liver.

I now teach filmmaking, and use "grassroots" quite a bit. It makes sense to me. You start with only what you've got, from the ground up. You rally some friends and work towards a common goal, without the motivation of money. All that rah-rah stuff. The money will come later. Students need to hear about that stuff. They need to hear they can go at it alone, in Michigan.

I still live in Grand Rapids. I still make movies with the same people. We're shooting another one next month. Michigan is where I make my movies. This is where I pay $400, all utilities included, on a killer apartment in a fancy part of town. This is where I can survive on a filmmaker's paycheck. This is where my people are.

Inside Perspective of an Encouraged Interloper

by Allison Manville Metz

In all honesty, before I joined the faculty at Grand Valley State University in 2009, Michigan had never been on my radar as a place to live, let alone knowing that a specific area called "West Michigan" even existed. I grew up in a central New Jersey suburb outside of New York City, lived in Austin, Texas, during its major tech boom at the turn of the century, and called Madison, Wisconsin, home (twice) for a total of twelve years.

"Oh, I have a [insert family member here] that loves Grand Rapids!" I heard from multiple sources, when I told people I was going to be a Grand Rapidian. When I followed up by asking exactly what they loved about Grand Rapids, the response almost always started out along the lines of "It's beautiful."

The Grand Rapids area of West Michigan is beautiful. Bright blue skies that seem to flaunt the cleanliness of air filtering in from nearby Lake Michigan. Neighborhoods that show off lush green midwestern grass that underscores a vibrant diversity of flowers, thanks to an abundance of precipitation, some of the most total rain and snow for any city in the United States. Many residents seem to forget about all the "lake effect" snowstorms and cloudy days during the glow of late-night summer sunsets on this western most edge of the eastern time zone.

For an outsider, such as myself, it took several years of living here before I was able to delineate unique aspects of this area of the Midwest. Many locals would explain away incidents with "Oh, that is so West Michigan!" before I understood what the shorthand reference meant. The amount of people in the area with V surnames and abundant tulips in their yards are a giveaway that West Michigan was settled by the Dutch many years ago. Politically conservative traditions and values govern most of the area. Like cities I had lived in before, Grand Rapids was a politically left-leaning oasis surrounded by die-hard right-wing counties. Christianity dominates the population's religious beliefs; it really is hard to throw a rock without hitting a church, and "Blue Laws" ruled the land so recently that even mowing your lawn on a Sunday could garner a disapproving glare from a neighbor. Not even two decades after being forbidden to buy groceries on a Sunday, Grand Rapids has become the self-proclaimed "Beer City, USA" with no end of new brewery establishments in sight. And there is no dearth of places to buy that beer, even on Sundays.

It takes some time after moving to this city to see past the natural beauty and conservatively calm Dutch influence in order to zoom in on the blemishes that mark up the socio-cultural landscape. Grand Rapids comes across to many of us non-natives as a "closed community" where local businesses hire who they know over who is most qualified and conversations suddenly end if you answer "None" when asked, "What church do you belong to?" Racially segregated neighborhood lines are drawn abruptly and severely and may change dramatically from one block to the next. It seems like Grand Rapids is a community that has no idea how to intermingle people with differing skin pigmentation and even when large groups of individuals are brought together through area universities or public events, there is automatic self-segregation—people flock to others that look like them. Most public schools in Grand Rapids are failing due to overcrowded classrooms, under-experienced teachers who can't be retained long enough to gain proper experience, and insufficient funding.

Since moving here in 2009, Grand Rapids has steadily become more prominent in the national consciousness. Both major political party presidential candidates came to Grand Rapids on Election Day in 2016. The city now consistently shows up on a number of "Top Ten" lists in recent years that rate places to live and, allegedly, Grand Rapids is currently the best city in the country to buy rental properties as the renovation business and new construction booms. The financial investments into the city bring all the growing pains and problems that come with catering to more of a white-collar population: gentrification threatens to run out poor, working-class families of color that have called Grand Rapids home for generations. If this growth trend continues, Grand Rapids will have to become more welcoming to people who bring outside perspectives into this white, Dutch, Christian conservative city in order for this place to continue to develop and thrive. The city will also have to figure out how to stop displacing the working poor and poverty stricken residents so that we all can proudly tell anyone who asks:

"Grand Rapids is a beautiful city in all sorts of ways for all sorts of people who live there."

Our History and Our Legacies

...where we unpack the power struggles of the past

Totentanz

by Stelle Slootmaker

we dancing Death at the end of the world.
no not a slow dance—
a go go go dance.

frenetic and senseless.

a bought and sold dance,
over the counter and under the table.
wheeled and dealt, bullshitted, targeted, marketed
by prescription and by-line;
(bi-partisan timelines track profits, build skylines.)

we dancing Death at the end of the world.
no not a dull dance
a full dance, a so full that
we can't stop dance.

apoplectic and tenseless.

a forgetting the past dance, disregarding the future.
'til Earth striking back black as night—
puts out the light
electric, human.

Skip to my Lou.
Skip to my Lou, my darling.

While this poem expresses how humanity is rushing towards a catastrophic finale, my hope is that it inspires us to step aside from this death dance and take time to imagine and create life, love, honest connections and respect for each other and Mother Earth. Another world is possible.

When Story is Thicker than Blood
by Marjorie Steele

Two hundred years ago, when the spring floods would recede from the banks of the Grand River, where present-day Grand Rapids goes about its daily urban bustle, the first objects to re-emerge from the waters were the rounded peaks of three dozen unnatural mounds. Ranging in size from minor knolls to sculpted three-story summits, these minor megaliths performed this dance for unknown thousands of years: rising from the dangerous rushing waters silently, and in unison, as a sign to the people living there that the chaotic destruction of winter and spring was giving way to creation once again.

Did these mounds reflect the patterns of star constellations their ancient builders revered, telling the story of cosmic origins and lingering connection? Were they placed to replicate the global map of a civilization that was wiped away in a past too distant for modern memory to fathom? Were they simply burial mounds made by native tribes to honor the dead, built higher over centuries with layers of dead kings and queens?

Or perhaps all of the above?

Today, less than a dozen mounds remain, clothed in hardwoods, tucked just out of sight of downtown Grand Rapids's southernmost Pearl Street Bridge. These are known as the "Norton Mounds," after the Captain Norton who owned the land upon which they rest until the late 1800s. The damming of the Grand River during Grand Rapids's industrialization has long since ceased the mounds' annual creation dance with the river's floodplain, and they stand dry and sequestered, like guardians, on the southern border of the city which is largely unaware of their existence.

Before the Midwest was colonized, these mounds were not unique to Grand Rapids—or even to the Midwest. The large mounds along the Grand River belonged to a pattern of an untold number of mounds which used to proliferate the state's landscape. Through both indifference and curiosity, however, the last 150 years have seen all but a fraction of these mounds razed, leaving little or no evidence behind. The mounds were points of great interest to gentlemen explorers, who took up the hobby of "excavating" these sacred sites with tenacity throughout the 1800s. When the treasure-hunting waned, farmers leveled mounds to make way for fields, and real estate magnates demolished them to make way for grocery stores.

Four major excavations have been performed on the Norton Mounds alone, with nearly fifty mounds in the modern-day Grand Rapids area surveyed, excavated, or both in the late 1800s. Western science has taken artifacts and remains from the mounds at will, but has yet to produce conclusive answers to the questions of who built these mounds, and for what purpose.

Common wisdom among the scientific community dates the "Hopewellian" culture to which the mounds are attributed from around 200 B.C. to A.D. 500 and dates the Norton Mounds to be at least 2,000 years old, but the evidence upon which these dates are based is arguably indeterminate. Some human remains within the mounds can be loosely dated, but dating the construction of the structures themselves—or understanding the method of construction—is another story. The artifacts, which give evidence of technology and civilization that are far more advanced than recorded history can account for, only raise more questions.

Stone pipes carved into animal likenesses in exquisite detail proliferate the mounds. Threaded stone tools, unlike any artifacts found in known Native American cultures—or any other ancient culture, for that matter—are scattered within the mounds like fragmented clues.

But the real twist, as always, comes down to blood.

Local scientific lore rumors that the DNA samples taken from human remains found within Grand Rapids's Hopewellian mounds have produced no linear connection with any Native American tribe known in Michigan.

Yet there is one thread that binds the builders of the mounds to local native tribes—a thread which is, in a way, stronger than blood: the oral histories of local Potawatomi-Ottowa tribes reference the builders of the mounds as their ancestors. Over the years, these frayed threads of oral history have mixed with rumors, hoaxes, and inconclusive data to weave some tantalizing tales.

Foreign tribes usurping a native culture; newcomers driving "giants" from the land; divine floods that cleansed the lands from an ancient race of people—fables like these hover around Hopewellian mythology like moths around a porch light.

Mystique and rumors aside, the story of what's happened to the mounds over the last 150 years is very real. While the vast majority near Grand Rapids have been destroyed—with modern monuments like Millennium Park and Ah-Nab-Awen Park (named and designed in homage to the Converse Mounds which used to stand there) taking their place, the Norton Mounds still stand, touched by research but not destroyed, largely unknown to the local public.

If these mounds stand as guarding monuments to the area, they themselves have seen their share of guardians over the years, protecting them from the fate of their many sisters—and protecting the secrets they contain for future generations.

In the early sixties, as development contracts for downtown Grand Rapids's highway construction were solidifying, the remaining Norton Mounds were a hair's breadth away from being dozed beneath the path of the new 196 freeway. Local tribes joined forces with the University of Michigan's researchers to protect the site, and managed to shift the path of construction to leave the mounds untouched. The sixties also saw the University of Michigan's formal excavation of the Norton Mounds—the last excavation to be performed on the mounds, during which a large sampling of human remains were taken.

Yet for all the scientific study that had been done, the mounds were megaliths without a people, until the work of Debra Muller in the early 2000s.

In her adulthood, Debra dug deeply into her Potawatomi-Ottowa ancestry—an ancestry which had almost been lost to her, having been adopted by a white family at birth. She was a prominent member of the Nottawaseppi Huron Band of the Potawatomi Nation, a chairwoman and commissioner with the City of Grand Rapids, founder of the Theatre of the Three Fires; the list goes on. Debra was a crusader for preserving Native American traditions for future generations—including the wealth of knowledge and story which tread much further, and deeper, into history than western scientific explanation can muster.

She directed the Norton Mounds project for the Grand Rapids Public Museum, the predecessor of the Kent Scientific Institute, which had funded Coffinbury's invasive excavation in the late 1800s. But the nature of Debra's work with the museum was fundamentally different: it was of creation, rather than destruction.

Working with both academic and native communities, Debra collected an exhaustingly comprehensive narrative of the mounds' known past, excavations, cultural origins, and, importantly, a vision for their future in the community. In 2003, Debra authored a comprehensive book, The Norton Mounds Site: A Description and History of a Prominent Cultural National Historic Landmark, followed in 2007 by a companion piece, which maps out a plan for landscape management of the site.

In 2010, the Public Museum voluntarily returned a host of artifacts—including human remains—taken from the mounds back to local native tribes. Unlike before, the twist here came down to story.

It wasn't DNA samples or carbon dating which allowed the museum to take action under the Native American Graves Protection and Repatriation Act and return ancestral remains to local tribes: it was the thread of oral history. The thread which Debra had found and restored with a dedication that ran deeper than blood.

Cancer took Debra's life less than one year later, her guardianship having made an indelible, if silent, mark on Grand Rapids's landscape.

Who will step next into the role of guardian of the traditions and secrets these mounds represent remains to be seen, but one thing is certain: the future of the Norton Mounds will require more skill with story than with a spade.

A Lesser Democracy

by Jeffrey D. Kleiman

The summer of 1911 witnessed the largest, most disruptive labor unrest in the history of Grand Rapids. The strike by furniture workers lasted six months, dividing the town along lines of class, religion, and ethnicity. Unaccustomed to demands for collective bargaining and widespread protest, the city's powerful business elite reacted to this challenge of authority in the workplace. The events following that strike summer provide valuable lessons today, more than a century later. One of the key points to recognize is how people in a democracy may actually subvert or weaken that democracy in the hopes of elevating "order" and "efficiency" to the principal values.

Municipal government in Grand Rapids, Michigan, began as a traditional form of strong mayor and city council, basing their actions on a direct voice from local ward and precinct voters along with the citywide selection of the mayor. However, under the leadership of the business elite, focused in the dominant furniture industry, government moved away from a robust democracy to a more limited level of representative government. This hallmark transition took place after the Great Strike of 1911. These selfsame industrialists felt that too much political power, along with the ability of ordinary workers to challenge their leadership through labor disruption, had to stop. To these ends, by 1916, furniture manufacturers and their allies worked hard to change the basic form and function of city government, effectively reducing the voice of many residents.

This obsession with maintaining order and stability stemmed from the very nature of the furniture industry itself. Planning for production required assessment of costs for raw materials, machinery, skilled labor, transportation, and shifts in market demands. As early as 1880, furniture manufacturing had become "by far the most important industry" in Grand Rapids and soon became the "recognized center of the furniture industry in the United States." Annual furniture market trade fairs brought more than 1,500 buyers by 1900 with increases each year thereafter. The furniture industry raised the city far above its national rank in terms of population. Compared on the basis of furniture manufacturing alone, Grand Rapids stood head to head with America's five largest cities.

Much of this strength derived from the collusion among the city's industrialists to stifle local competition and create their own locally-owned banks to deal with capital needs. Long- and short-term investment loans soon originated from a series of new banks chartered after 1905, where the furniture men filled the boards of directors and other officers. These men often pledged their factories as collateral to insure repayment of their loans along with their capital assets: machinery, raw materials, building expansion. Here, they were able to grant themselves loans on the most favorable terms while pledging their business property to the bank (effectively themselves and colleagues). This interlocking directorate extended beyond banking interests to include each other's businesses.

Workers found themselves further enmeshed in this system if they owned a home. Grand Rapids boasted a rate of homeownership far above the national average by the turn of the century, suggesting that many household incomes beyond the wage-dependent furniture worker went to acquire real property. Given that one-third of all employees in the city labored for the furniture industry, the control exercised by manufacturers over mortgages granted by banks or savings and loans institutions (dominated by the manufacturers) only enhanced the necessity to accept working conditions and wages as offered.

The city's leading industrialists created a privately funded Employers Association in 1905 to help place workers in the various plants around town. However, the association maintained a central card index that listed all workers, skill levels, and wages; with such a resource, no manufacturer might overpay a worker and foster dangerous competition among the industrialists, thus deranging the stability of wage levels as part of cost containment. One example of this control concerned a disgruntled wage earner leaving one employer to seek work with another. He had received $2 per day on his former job. Asking for $2.25 per day without mentioning his former employer or wage level, the association told the applicant that $2 was all he had received and might hope to receive. Likely any complaint from him would have resulted in becoming part of an industrial blacklist that noted people who were no longer "competent or worthy" to work in town.

Thus, wage earners who had already committed themselves to a longer-term debt in the form of a mortgage (usually renewable every one to three years) found themselves with deepened dependence on the city's industrial leadership. Attempts to challenge the manufacturers could result in blacklisting: no job, no income, no home. By the time of the strike in 1911, the Grand Rapids furniture workers had become involuntary partners in financing companies they worked for, but consistently denied any voice in determining wages, hours, or working conditions.

Worker unrest in the furniture industry had been building, though, for some time. As far back as 1909, a three-man committee, representing forty-five skilled cabinetmakers out of a workforce of more than 300, asked management at the Oriel factory for a cost-of-living increase. The request for wages came as a response to inflation. One sign of the jump, obvious to most working men, came with the disappearance of the popular $0.15 dinners. On the whole this request appeared quite reasonable and modest. One of the city's aldermen had even advocated a boycott to drive down food prices. All the local papers remarked on the increased cost of food.

Rather than recognize the legitimacy of the need, the plant owner fired the men as "agitators" in January 1910—two months after their initial meeting. By October of that year, 4,000 workers across the city organized informally and voted to request changes in the piece-rate system along with increased wages and shorter hours. Effectively making their point with a brief walkout in December, promises came from one of the key factory owners that "beyond question, after the first of the year [1911], what they requested would be granted." However, that employees wanted a say in the terms of their employment was an unthinkable precedent that owners sought to avoid at all costs.

The citywide Furniture Manufacturers Association circulated a letter among the entire 6,000 plus workforce stating that the traditional policy of each firm had been always to recognize "the liberty of every man, union or nonunion, without discrimination, to sell his labor freely, independently, and at the best price obtainable." No mention appeared of the Employers Association that tracked all workers and wages. Nor had the presence of unions among the industrial wage earners been mentioned until this point. Francis Campau, representing the Employers Association, asserted that workers already received first-class treatment in terms of wages and hours, noting that the nine-hour day was practically a reality given that Saturday was only a half-day. There were no grounds for complaints, only an unwarranted interference by workers into the affairs of private business.

The *Evening News* called upon the manufacturers to yield some ground. Increased wages helped more than workers, it helped to grow the entire city economy. "The general well-being of the many," lectured the paper, "in proportion as the purchasing power of the great wage-earning classes increases or lessens, so must wax or wane the prosperity of the business classes generally." The editorial maintained that higher wages would raise the prosperity of all merchants and retailers by putting more money into the hands of consumers. Pushing for low wages and longer hours only dampened the whole cycle of economic growth. Therefore, why not accede to the requests.

The manufacturers held firm. Tensions mounted across Grand Rapids as a gathering of several thousand workers met at the end of March 1911 and voted overwhelmingly to strike come April 1. In the wake of this popular support, the Evening Press condemned the businessmen's intransigence, excoriating them by writing that "the attitude as to WHAT IS YOUR BUSINESS AND WHAT IS OUR BUSINESS has altered. The conclusion has been reached that anything which affects OUR safety, our happiness and our pocketbooks, like a strike, is very much the public business."

As the strike deadline loomed, a citizen's committee composed of manufacturers, religious leaders, and community leaders formed to seek a compromise. Despite the hopes of a peaceful resolution, after more than a week, the committee reported that nothing had changed. The bottom line, quite literally, came from the furniture men who stated unequivocally that there would never be any form of collective bargaining permitted. *They* owned the businesses, *they* controlled all aspects of the production process, and workers could only sell their labor at the rate manufacturers would pay. Take it or leave it. Workers walked out on April 19, effectively bringing production to a standstill.

Fearful of violence, the city's most popular mayor, George Ellis, organized workers to keep themselves busy by organizing baseball games and in good standing by convincing them to keep fellow strikers out of the bars. As a measure of support, bar owners reduced their hours of operation, policed their customers to enforce limited drinking, if not abstinence, and tolerated the union pickets outside their doors. When violence threatened to erupt outside a furniture factory, Ellis would address crowds numbering in the hundreds, defusing the resentment, with most of the people walking away as many stayed behind to chat with him and shake his hand.

Increasingly, the furniture manufacturers viewed Ellis as an enemy, using the city government to advance the cause of workers rather than remain neutral. They threatened him by holding him accountable for any damage to their property. They demanded police protection for the small numbers who still showed up to work. And if Ellis did not act to remove picketing strikers outside factory gates, then they would find their own means "in self-defense" to protect these loyal employees "through such lawful sources as are open to us." The popular mayor and, by extension, the city government, had become the greatest threat to the furniture industrialists' control.

These fears came to fruition in mid-May, when violence erupted around the west side furniture factories. On the late afternoon of May 15, crowds began to gather outside the Widdicomb factories, surrounding owner Harry Widdicomb's car as he tried to enter the factory gates. Bricks, stones, sticks, and anything handy pelted the car—reports of pistol shots in the melee only intensified the violence. One protesting mother put down her child to attack a policeman. As the numbers increased over the next few hours, the narrow streets became dangerously impassable. Local fire companies appeared to break up the rioters by spraying them with fire hoses; after ten minutes, they left, clearly having failed to disrupt the crowds.

Mayor Ellis came to the site, hoping to restore calm, encouraging the strikers, their families, and others, to disperse. After entering the factory gates to talk with Harry Widdicomb, he emerged, raised his hands in a call for silence. "The crowds came forward like an orderly audience," noted the paper. "One man shouted 'We'll believe Ellis anytime, but we won't let those coppers come around bossing us.'" Faced with an orderly, disciplined gathering of angry residents, Ellis pleaded for peace. Some drifted away, only to return after Ellis's departure. As darkness fell, rioters lined both sides of the street in order to bombard the factory with stones, debris, bricks, or anything that might be hurled at the factory windows. By midnight, every window had been shattered.

Finally, thirty club-wielding policemen pushed forward, breaking up the protesters' crowd. Police arrested a few demonstrators and began a retreat from the area. Using the prisoners as shields, the policemen fired their weapons into the air until they ran out of ammunition. Hand-to-hand battles ensued and rioters threatened to overcome the police until reinforcements appeared. Newspaper accounts painted the picture of "the street [being] filled with madly running and cursing men and women" with "almost every other face...streaked with blood from an injury or from the injury of another. Mayor Ellis turned up again for the second time that night to urge the throng to head home. They cheered Ellis, but remained unmoved, staunchly determined to persist in their angry protest.

The next morning, city papers reported on the west side violence. In a move to promote worker responsibility for keeping the future peace, Ellis created a series of peace patrols composed of strikers. These men walked the factory district, assuring that there would be no further repeats of large crowds to assail factory owners or attack the factories. The benefits here to the striking workers were twofold: by demonstrating responsibility in the protection of person and private property, they established credibility for wage earners in the city. Former President Theodore Roosevelt praised these peace patrols, proclaiming that "Such working men show themselves not only good citizens whose patriotism takes a practical form, but also the wisest kind of advocates for advancing the cause of the wage earner." Additionally, welcome were the small sums paid to the peace patrols that helped sustain households during the growing period without a regular income.

Strikers persisted throughout the summer, despite growing doubts along with the continued need to feed families and pay rent. Yet the pressures continued to grow until more than 2,000 workers voted to return to the factories under the old, pre-strike conditions. Hopes for any shared voice in the workplace fell with their response. By the end of August, strikers conceded defeat, returning to those plants where the employers would have them.

This strike summer of 1911 and the attendant violence convinced manufacturers that they could not trust city government to safeguard their factories or protect replacement workers. Even more ominously, the confrontation only hardened positions by owners and workers. The longer term effects appeared as the manufacturers, in alliance with other bankers and businessmen, determined to alter the structure of city government in order to enhance their political control and influence, reflecting their outsized economic role. Beginning in 1912, Grand Rapids's business elite mounted a municipal reform movement aimed at creating a city government that effectively concentrated power in the hands of business leaders.

Economic hardship in the years 1913-1914 provided the environment for industrialists to make a serious push for such profound reform. As part of an unofficial relief program to help the increasing numbers of unemployed, Mayor Ellis used city resources to create jobs. He did this through inter-fund borrowing, taking unused portions from one department and disbursing the funds elsewhere; parks and street repair provided temporary work for the needy and indigent. While such procedures anticipated strategies later adopted by local governments during the Great Depression, many contemporary critics viewed them as an irresponsible use of municipal budgets.

At the heart of this reform stood the notion that American cities should be governed in a modern, efficient, businesslike way. Progressive reforms proposed that professional managers would administer cities under the direction of commissioners. Uninvolved with day-to-day decisions, managers had tolerated gambling, drinking, and prostitution. Experts, rather than political appointees, could hold sway. Diluting voter influence, the 1916 Charter reduced the number of city wards from twelve to three, reducing the ratio of local representation to population. The three wards effectively diluted immigrant and working-class votes by mixing them in among competing ethnic groups. The new city council would be limited to seven members, two from each of the new wards and one elected citywide.

In a break with the past, all these posts would be conducted as at-large elections. This meant that a candidate who lived in a wealthier neighborhood could run to represent the interests of the poorer ones. Candidates with greater resources, economic and organizational, might very well gain the advantage of a local one. Such an advantage emerged as a critical one now that the new wards were so much larger and diverse. By giving the city commission power over the direct appointment or approval of municipal officials, that charter made the commissioners alone the ultimate dispensers of another variety of patronage. This further removed the popular voice from city management by taking away the assurance that local representation from the ward and precinct level might be heard. As it happened, and as it was intended to happen, the concentration of political power fell to the richest residents—businessmen and their allies who held a four-seat majority in the new council once the charter became effective in 1917. The mayoral office remained in place only due to the fact that state law prohibited its removal; however, it became a figurehead position, largely ceremonial, devoid of any effective executive power. Along with the loss of political power expressed directly in the new configuration of council and mayor, the business reformers undercut informal political influence by eliminating the practice of patronage.

Rather than finding employment secured appointments by the mayor or aldermen for allies and families, or creating work in a variety of city projects, all municipal employees were subjected to civil service examinations. However, civil service reform as laid out in the new city charter did not put an end to political patronage, it merely changed the pool of acceptable patronage recipients and eliminated brokering between the mayor and alderman over appointments to city hall. Civil service exams favored the educated applicants who were versed in mathematics, the English language, and organizational skills. The children of immigrants might aspire to these posts, but only the educated would be able to compete.

The "noncompetitive" category of municipal positions required "peculiar and exceptional qualifications of a scientific, managerial, professional or educational character as may be determined" by the governing commission. This opened up the opportunity of municipal administrative employment for the well-educated sons of industrialists, bankers, and lawyers, rather than those of factory workers or the children of immigrants. By giving the city commission power over the direct appointment or approval of municipal officials, that charter made the commissioners alone the ultimate dispensers of another variety of patronage.

Yet, in order to become the new governmental vehicle in Grand Rapids, the charter required a majority vote. How and why would factory workers and other wage-dependent men vote to reduce their own access to democratic government and

influence on those elected to office? A close look at ward and precinct patterns tells the story. One major factor contributing to the
endorsement of this reform was the high degree of home ownership in the city. The commitment to home ownership, along with
the family life it represented, fostered a fear of disruption and loss.

The 1916 businessmen's charter stressed a promise of stability for aspiring middle-class families, those recently established
and those who hoped to climb the ladder. Its advocates argued
that such stability could be best achieved through efficient, businesslike administration of municipal affairs. By accepting this
emphasis on the security of property, homeowners across the
city found common cause with the industrialists. Given the context of local politics, the manufacturers' program of reform presented voters with an alternative strategy for preserving their
material gains while participating in the political process. The
irony was that workers contributed to their own political exclu-
sion by voting for this new form of government.

The strike and subsequent charter revision remain relevant.
Despite the fact that the strikers outnumbered factory owners
and that many in the city supported the strikers' demands, the
concentration of wealth in the hands of the city's elite allowed
them to outlast the workers. Their smaller numbers also gave
them a greater ability to organize in a consistent manner, a tactic ill-suited to the sprawling and ethnically diverse furniture
workers. This same level of organization, along with financial resources, permitted the city's elite to pursue political reform that
served their own best interests.

The great lesson here is that the ordinary wage earners and
many other small business owners sided with this new government. They read the promise of social stability and professional business management as keys to protecting their
hard won gains; homeowners and others who aspired to social
mobility endorsed this concentration of power. These voters
viewed the new government as the only way to curb the exces-
sive influence of the "wrong" sorts of people. While we today
may wonder why so many people voted against their apparent

self-interest in reducing their access to government, it may be instructive to ask how they defined their self-interest. And the briefest answer may very well be: hold the other fellows at bay, keep the local economy stable, and safeguard private property.

This piece was excerpted from Strike!: How the Furniture Workers Strike in 1911 Changed Grand Rapids *(2006) with permission from Grand Rapids Historical Commission.*

The History of Midtown
by Matthew Russell

Grand Rapids is a big little town.

It's a favorite conversation starter for taxi drivers, and seemingly the best way to describe both our neighborly attitudes and metropolitan aspirations.

But while Grand Rapids expands upward and outward, its foundation is yet influenced heavily by history. The neighborhoods of Grand Rapids are each distinct in their own way, reflecting a variety of cultural histories, economic changes, successes, and failures.

Modern-day Midtown, with a population of just over 4,000, according to 2013 Community Research Institute (CRI) figures, is bordered to the north by I-196, to the east by Fuller Street, to the south by Fulton, and to the west by Union. It's one of the oldest and most venerated neighborhoods in Grand Rapids and is just as tethered to historical events as its neighboring communities.

The Midtown Neighborhood Association is currently one of the most effective and active associations in the city, but as with every other neighborhood in Grand Rapids, its roots are based in civil unrest. The 1911 Furniture Strikes saw the interests of blue-collar westsiders clashing with those of the wealthy factory owners on the east side of the Grand River. And a government once led by mayoral autocracy, where paid aldermen represented the concerns of eleven different wards, was fractured into the current city charter, which allowed room for thirty-two unfunded neighborhood associations in three wards.

The new rules were not entirely designed to represent citizen interests, however, favoring industrial expansion over citizens and sustainability.

The cycle of privilege reinforced an inequitable system, and it's impossible to define the characteristics of any neighborhood in Grand Rapids without taking that cycle into consideration. But that's not to say the citizenry of our fair city has been stifled by setback. Conflict begets progress, and Midtown is not outside that loop.

Foundation

As the name "Brikyaat," the northeastern portion of the neighborhood, implies, Midtown owes no small part of its history to Dutch workers. Nearly 125 years ago, the Banner of Truth, a publication based in New York City, heralded the beginnings of what was to come in West Michigan. The seeds and early growth of European settlement are detailed in clippings found filed away on the fourth floor of the Grand Rapid Public Library.

"A new Holland congregation was organized in the Grand Rapids Brickyard on Monday, February 6, 1893," the Banner reported.

Henry Ippel, professor of history, emeritus, at Calvin College, and former field agent for the Historical Committee of the Christian Reformed Church, cited the same article in his detailed history of "The Brickyard: A Dutch Neighborhood in Grand Rapids," a presentation he made by the same name to colleagues a century later.

"Already in 1852, the demand for bricks in the growing city encouraged the establishment of a brick factory utilizing the clay found on the eastern fringe of the city," Ippel wrote in 1993.

He continued, "Shortly after the Civil War, more factories were formed, one by three Dutch entrepreneurs: Martin Klaasen, Anthony De Heus, and Frank Overbeek. By 1890 there were three substantial brick and tile manufacturers listed in the city directory, and five years later these companies were united into the Grand Rapids Consolidated Brick and Tile Company, which survived into the twentieth century."

A concentration of "kilns, storage sheds, and clay pits" lent the name to the area we know today as the Brikyaat Neighborhood.

Alongside the Woods, Coldbrook Creek, Cegeilnia Crossings, Ashby Row, the Old East End, and North of Market, these districts make up what we know as Midtown.

Connection

As reported in the Grand Rapids Evening News on Aug. 17, 1901, "The 'by the brickyard' settlement extending from the East Fulton Street cemetery nearly to North Fuller Street and bounded by Fountain and Fulton Streets probably contains more houses, more inhabitants, and more children to the square than any other residence district in Grand Rapids."

The article reports that "The houses on the narrow courts and alleys are so close together that in many cases if a busy housewife should discover that she was out of tea she could borrow from a neighbor without leaving the house."

Compared to a beehive on a summer's day, the neighborhood detailed in the Evening News continued to swell and recycle itself into further prosperity for decades to come. And on most of those days, nowhere else in Midtown will you find a greater collection of locals milling about with their neighbors than at the Fulton Street Farmers Market (FSFM).

"Aside from being the primary marketplace in the area, I think that the market brings in all sorts of clientele to the area and hopefully in return, they also shop at the other businesses in the Midtown neighborhood," says market manager Rori Weston. "I believe that the Farmers Market's role in the neighborhood is bringing forth a common place for the neighbors to gather and shop for local food."

Founded in 1922, its land being purchased from James Langdon Mckee that year for $1,900, the FSFM was initially monikered the "East Side Market," the oldest and largest of the four public farmers markets that have been in operation within Grand Rapids. For decades, its tables and tarps endured prosperity and depression. The office building as seen from Fulton Street was even once a diner between 1953 and 1955.

By the twenty-first century, it was obvious the market had fallen into disrepair. A rebuilding campaign, with Midtown serving as the contractor, helped create the beautiful and farmer-friendly market aisles and outpost we know today.

"My earliest memory of the market was back in 2008 when the market was just tarps and tables," says Weston. "I have some fond memories walking down the tiny aisle with barely any room to move and my arms full of produce to feast on."

As it was then, and still is today, the market is a place of community engagement, wellness, and love, Weston says.

Notes filed by agrifood scholar Jayson Otto in 2011 at the Grand Rapids Public Library indicate that residents of the Midtown area had been petitioning the city of Grand Rapids for its creation at least five years prior to its founding. And as it does today, the market owes much of its success to dedicated and politically active women, who took on leadership of the market's creation after previous attempts to move street peddlers to a common market had failed.

For ninety-five years, the market has provided a seam where rural and urban West Michiganders share stories, interests, and fresh produce. No small number of the vendors that operate within the stalls today are the second or third generation of families that had helped make it so popular in the twentieth century.

As many as 6,000 visitors may walk through the FSFM on a summer Saturday, more than doubling the population of Midtown as a whole. For those few hours, there are more than just new friendships being made, there is history.

"I have always had sense of belonging to this space," Weston says. "It was about the farmers and the friends who came together each Saturday, week after week."

Growth

By the 1950s, the Dutch population of Midtown and their business interests had waned. The community built, quite literally, upon a foundation of bricks, tempered by austerity and the Dutch Reformed Church, was passed on to other Grand Rapidians returning home from World War II.

Today you can find people of nearly every race, ethnicity, and nationality in the world represented in Midtown, and expansion happening seemingly on every corner. One of the clearest signs of growth and social prosperity, according to Midtown resident, former Midtown Neighborhood Association Board Member, and current West Michigan Environmental Action Council (WMEAC) President Christine Helms-Maletic, is the variety of restaurants.

"When we first moved here you couldn't find a vegetarian restaurant besides Gaia within a twenty-minute drive," says Helms-Maletic. "Now I can walk to my ten favorite restaurants in town. I think that's the biggest change. The neighborhood business districts have made huge strides since then."

Even before Little Africa, and Kitchens Curry and Kangaroo came to town, Midtown's location made it the epicenter of action for anyone wanting a walkable neighborhood.

Helms-Maletic says when she and her husband first came to Grand Rapids by way of Bloomington, Indiana, in 1997, they nearly bought the first house they saw. The second one, they didn't pass by.

"I walked by it and said, that's the house for us. We made an offer the same day," she says. "I loved the neighborhood. I loved the fact that you could walk to the library, the farmers market, or downtown. At the time, the [YMCA] was still the Y. The location was very appealing."

Midtown businesses continue to branch out and expand, and perhaps none so fittingly represent the diligence and industriousness of our neighborhood's roots than those of Kameel Chamelly. Chamelly founded Martha's Vineyard as a wine shop at 200 Union Avenue in 1981. Today, along with Nantucket Baking Company and the Lyon Street Café, Chamelly's patrons are finding much more than wine at the corner of Lyon and Union. The intersection has become a meeting place for friends from all over the city, and a landmark stop-of-all-trades for Midtown residents.

While Michigan Street has seen the most construction over the last year, Fulton Street is turning a corner as well, Helms-Maletic says. But that's not to say all forms of expansion are healthy.

"We're starting to see more occupancy in our district, but I also think the high demand can drive up prices, and then you don't have the same level of opportunity for everyone, and that's concerning," she says.

Today, someone may put their house on the market and see it sold within three days, Helms-Maletic says, which is encouraging to those who own their own homes, but such economic trends aren't as kind on renters.

"To me, renters keep a neighborhood vibrant," she says. "It's important to have a good mix of owners and renters. That brings in a good mix of income, a good mix of ages, a good mix of races and ethnic backgrounds. To me, that's a good neighborhood."

While the disparity between owners and renters is a concern throughout the city of Grand Rapids, the differences in those demographics based on race are even more alarming. As Michigan Radio's State of Opportunity reporter Dustin Dwyer wrote in "Pushed Out: A Documentary on Housing in Grand Rapids," at least 40 percent of the African Americans living in the city are below the poverty level, while half as many whites face the same economic challenges.

And as home prices rise, Dwyer notes, investors have been quick to buy up foreclosed properties throughout the city, driving prices up even further. Kent County data indicates that investors hold ownership to 45 percent of the homes that experienced foreclosure between 2008 and 2016.

Organization

Shortly after moving to Midtown in the nineties, Helms-Malefic got involved with the neighborhood association alongside previous staffer Kelly Otto, a dynamic force of community building in her own right. Through her work with the association board, and her experiences as an educator, Helms-Malefic was tapped to offer project consultation during the FSFM capital campaign in 2011, launching her current career in the field.

But while the neighborhood's roots can be traced back to civil unrest, the neighborhood association's beginnings aren't that dissimilar.

"It is a fact of life that political activism only happens when something goes wrong," Midtown resident Julie Stivers says in *Heart and Soul: The Story of Grand Rapids Neighborhoods*, by Linda Samuelson and Andrew Schrier.

What went wrong once stood on the current footprint of Midtown Green Park at the corner of Fountain and Eastern.

The Baxter Laundry building, left vacant and crumbling in the mid-seventies, was getting little attention from the city, despite the warnings of a group of concerned citizens.

Following a fire in the building that left the neighboring homes covered in soot and ash, this group took on the name FUMD (Fulton, Union, Michigan, and Diamond), and brought their heated issue to city leaders. They met regularly throughout the eighties, and as Community Development Block Grant funding became available in the nineties, eventually organized as the Midtown Neighborhood Association.

Diversity

When Midtown Neighborhood Association Board co-chair Mark Stoddard moved to Grand Rapids in the 1980s, and to Midtown in 1992, he says, most of his neighbors were in their seventies and eighties. The following decades saw the neighborhood renew itself as younger individuals and young families moved in, replacing those older neighbors.

"Many of these new residents have further invested in the neighborhood by renovating their homes and improving an already solid housing stock," says Stoddard. "The crime level has decreased over the years, and I've seen a sense of community grow between neighbors on a block—or, in the case of the Ashby Row sub-neighborhood of Midtown—grow between most residents within the sub-neighborhood."

The CRI data from 2013 list 71.3 percent of the Midtown population as white, an increase of 4.32 percent over the prior three years. African Americans have been attracted to Midtown in much higher numbers, making up 21.3 percent of the population in 2013, from 13.15 percent in 2000. Hispanics or Latinos have left Midtown in the greatest numbers, claiming 13.35 percent of the population in 2000, but just 2.7 percent three years later.

What sets Midtown apart from the other neighborhoods of the city, Stoddard says, is its economic diversity.

"Traditionally, no matter your income level, you could find a place to rent or buy within Midtown's boundaries," he says.

On the flip side of that coin, what sets Midtown apart from the other neighborhoods is that it is currently threatened by its own redevelopment along Michigan Street. Adding hundreds of market-priced apartments to the Michigan Street Corridor has raised costs of housing in the adjacent neighborhoods, and could filter out all but individuals and families of a certain income level.

"Midtown is working diligently to remind those at city hall and the developers working in our neighborhood of the need to focus on uses that do not weaken or destroy the fabric of Midtown and to help us to protect the economic diversity of our residents, which is a matter of pride among so many in Midtown," says Stoddard. "And the neighborhood association is working hard to build a sense of community amongst neighbors and a sense of pride in Midtown. These two components are crucial to the building and sustaining of a healthy neighborhood."

As a lawyer, Stoddard says he brings advocacy skills and an attention to detail to the Midtown Neighborhood Association. As a Midtown homeowner, he brings a desire to protect his investment in his home and the neighborhood.

"But as a twenty-five-year Midtown resident, I bring an enthusiasm, love for, and a commitment to, the neighborhood," he says. "Like most Midtown residents, I want to help make Midtown a place you want to come home to."

People have been coming home to Midtown for over a century and a half. The little brick-built corner of a larger city's story. And our neighborhood is all the richer for it.

An earlier version of this piece was published at Rapid Growth Media.

Grand Rapids Was a Part of the Central American Sanctuary Movement in the 1980s

by Jeff Smith

In the late 1970s and 1980s, US funded counter-insurgency wars were being waged in El Salvador and Guatemala. Activists along the US-Mexico border began to see a sharp rise in the number of political refugees entering the country.

As communities began to offer safety to these refugees, they realized that all of them had a similar narrative. Each of the refugees told them that they fled their country because they either witnessed the torture and murder of family members or they themselves were torture survivors.

The US-financed death squads in El Salvador and Guatemala were the primary source of the displacement of hundreds of thousands of people coming from Central America in the 1980s. US activists began to hear these stories in greater numbers, and since the Reagan administration did not acknowledge Salvadoran or Guatemalan refugees as being political refugees, the Central American Sanctuary Movement was born.

The Central American Sanctuary Movement was begun by US faith-based communities that believed that they should offer sanctuary for their fellow humans who were fleeing violence, even if it meant violating US laws.

Beginning in the southwestern part of the country, sanctuaries began popping up, where faith-based groups began to house people fleeing violence and provide them with a forum to tell their stories.

Soon there were hundreds of places declaring themselves a sanctuary for Central American refugees, with three places declaring in Michigan alone—Detroit, Lansing, and Grand Rapids.

The Grand Rapids Sanctuary was run by members of the Koinonia House, of which I was a part. The Koinonia House was a housing collective that had begun in 1984 and did much of their organizing around resisting US policy in Central

America. We had participated in numerous protests, marches, letter writing campaigns, and even engaged in civil disobedience at local Congressional offices. However, we all felt that something more needed to be done and we decided that we needed to use our collective privilege and take a stand in solidarity with those who had fled their countries because of the US-backed repression in El Salvador and Guatemala.

The seven of us, who were members of the Koinonia House, decided in the fall of 1985 to be part of the Central American Sanctuary Movement and traveled to Chicago to meet with the national coordinator of the project, the Chicago Religious Task Force on Central America.

One major aspect of becoming a sanctuary was the need for those seeking to declare themselves a sanctuary to obtain support from the community, especially in the form of letters. Such letters were a sign that Koinonia House would indeed be trusted with doing the work and it signaled to the federal authorities that those who signed the letters stood with the members of the Grand Rapids sanctuary. After soliciting letters, Koinonia House received dozens of endorsements from churches, community and university organizations, individuals, and parents with whom we had a relationship. Holy Trinity Episcopal Church was one of the organizations to endorse our efforts. Here is what they said:

> "We feel strongly this is the loving and compassionate response which the church should and must take in this situation, and sanctuary has long been established within the history and tradition of the church. So we support your compassionate and courageous stand, and are ready to support you in whatever way is possible."

Once the Koinonia House had significant community support for becoming a sanctuary, we set a date to declare ourselves a place that would defy the federal government and provide sanctuary to Central American refugees.

We declared ourselves a sanctuary in the fall of 1986 on the steps of the Gerald R. Ford Federal Building in downtown

Grand Rapids, as it was custom to make this declaration public. Members of the Detroit and Lansing Sanctuaries were present, with Fr. Dick Preston leading a ceremony to honor the public commitment being taken by our community.

Several months later, the Chicago Religious Task Force on Central America contacted us to let us know that they had two indigenous families from Guatemala in need of sanctuary.

In April of 1987, six adults and one child arrived in Grand Rapids at the Koinonia House. A few days later a press conference was held on the front porch of the Koinonia House and this marked the beginning of several years that the Grand Rapids sanctuary offered a safe haven for those who were fleeing violence in Central America.

Once the families arrived, we gave them time to get settled in. However, after a few weeks of becoming acclimated to West Michigan, we began organizing speaking opportunities for the Guatemalans living with us in sanctuary.

The Central American Sanctuary Movement had two main goals. First was the commitment to offer a safe place for people to live who were fleeing political violence. The second part of the work was to try to influence public opinion and eventually change the national policy around US support for the counter-insurgency wars in Central America.

We never fully knew how much we were under surveillance, but within the first month of offering sanctuary to the Guatemalans that had arrived, two FBI agents showed up one day at our door. Not knowing who they were, the Guatemalans let them in. However, there were several friends who had stopped by at that very moment and the FBI agents left, since there were so many people present. The only way we could truly keep those in sanctuary safe was to be as public about their presence as possible, which is why it was so important for them to share their stories in public.

Over the next several years, the families who were in sanctuary in Grand Rapids spoke on campuses, in churches, and at other community-based organizations. The Guatemalans shared personal stories and discussed how US policy was creating more terror and violence in their country. Speaking publicly for those in sanctuary in Grand Rapids was never an easy task. The Guatemalans who were in sanctuary in Grand Rapids spoke Qanjobal, one of twenty-three Mayan dialects. Therefore, those who spoke did so in Spanish, which was their second language. Quite often the Guatemalans in sanctuary would say that there are certain words in Qanjobal that didn't translate well, which made it difficult for them to articulate their experiences completely.

After a decade, the families were eventually able to gain legal status with the assistance of some amazing immigration lawyers. The two original families that were part of sanctuary had more children and those children are now approaching thirty years of age. In 1992, on October 12, Indigenous People's Day, we signed titles over to the Guatemalan families as a small way of making restitution for the 500 years of genocide that we all have benefitted from.

This organizing experience deeply affected me and I ended up doing solidarity work in Central America and Mexico over the next twenty years. Being part of the Central American Sanctuary Movement also taught me the power of direct action. Direct action moves beyond tactics that are symbolic or ineffective. Those of us who were part of this movement had to be willing to directly put our own lives at risk of government repression. This experience taught me that real change happens when we take risks and move beyond petitions and other symbolic tactics that only end up making us feel good. We had to practice deep solidarity by offering our home as a sanctuary and to provide opportunities for the Guatemalans in sanctuary to tell their stories that would move others to action.

It has been over thirty years since Grand Rapids had a sanctuary for those fleeing political violence from US-backed counterinsurgency warfare. During the George W. Bush and Barack Obama administrations, millions of undocumented immigrants were deported. With the Trump administration now in power, there is finally another movement beginning in Grand

Rapids that uses direct action and offers sanctuary to those who need it.

This current movement could adopt the philosophy from the 1980s Central American Sanctuary Movement, which believed in offering radical hospitality to those who were victims of US-backed repression. In addition, today's efforts should avoid creating bureaucratic structures, like nonprofits, and organize an autonomous, decentralized movement, which will be better equipped to meet the needs of the undocumented community. Having an autonomous, decentralized movement will make it more difficult for the state to engage in repression and target those involved.

Organizing for Abortion Rights

by John Nuerenberg

Women were being hassled and subjected to very unpleasant gestures and comments from the supposed "pro-life" camp. This included vulgar signs, physically blocking patients from entering women's clinics, and various legal attempts to restrict women from obtaining health care. Some women were seeking basic medical health care; others, an abortion. Grand Rapids was one of many cities in the later 1980s and the early 1990s that was hit by Operation Rescue. Operation Rescue is one of the leading pro-life Christian activist organizations in the nation. Being a national group, Grand Rapids was not spared from their activism, just like dozens of cities across the country.

In response, a woman and I worked together to form Pro-Choice Advocates of Greater Grand Rapids (PCA). Its mission was "to restore and advance reproductive freedom for every individual." PCA held numerous public speaking events and protest marches in Grand Rapids. One of our main purposes was to act as patient protectors against the Operation Rescue folks at the area women's health clinics. We also sold tee shirts with the PCA logo to further support our cause. PCA was also a member of a coalition for women's rights, the other members being National Organization for Women (NOW), National Abortion Rights Action League (NARAL), and Planned Parenthood. Even as part of a group, it was PCA that was the largest and most effective group promoting a woman's right to abortion.

Many times a clinic would call us and inform us of a "strike" by Operation Rescue or its local anti-choice affiliate. PCA garnered the support of more than 100 individuals, who were contacted by an organized phone tree developed by PCA and its volunteers. We could quickly gather twenty to fifty people to act as patient protectors at the affected clinic. Court injunctions were already in place for the anti-choice people to stay within so many feet of the clinic, but that didn't stop them. PCA members formed two parallel lines from the street, where patients were dropped off, to the front door of the clinic so as to allow patients space to proceed into the clinic in safety. PCA volunteers, being understanding and compassionate people to their issue, served not only as patient protectors, but as physical buffers from Operation Rescue "strikers."

PCA actively recruited volunteers of all races, genders, ages, and professions. We regularly had a large mixed assembly attend our events and patient protection actions. Our speakers were public officials, ministers, and activists. We received media attention from the Grand Rapids Press and many television interviews regarding our activities, purpose, and general awareness of our direction.

I remember one time a woman was leaving a clinic in a very pregnant state. She was being persecuted by the anti-choicers, both verbally and with signs being displayed in her face. She finally yelled out she just visited the clinic for a regular checkup and was planning to go full term and have her baby.

Several times we had to lock arms to keep the anti-choice folks from breaking our parallel lines. They were singing hymns and reading from the Bible while simultaneously crawling on their hands and knees to get between our legs. I felt like we were stopping some wild animal or dangerous insect from gaining access to their prey!

Our meetings at PCA were mostly attended by women. Once they got to know me, I was accepted as a leader in their cause. My wife and two daughters were behind me in my efforts but never attended a protest action at a clinic. I felt, and still do today, that there are several things that are best left to the individual, including having or not having an abortion. I have also been very vocal about other women's issues, such as equal pay for the same work and violence against women. PCA evolved into many other women's issues beyond abortion in the late 1990s while still pursuing its original purpose. To me, these issues are the substance of our humanness and I feel more strongly about women's issues than any other.

PCA grew and became stronger. Events were held in various venues, including Fountain Street Church, Rosa Parks Circle Park, and Calder Plaza. We held several protest marches on the downtown streets (sidewalks) of Grand Rapids around the Calder Plaza on Ottawa and Monroe Avenues and Pearl and Lyon Streets, and any other street that we were allowed on and protected by the police. The belief, which proved true, was that we were effectively educating many in the public as well as successfully helping the clinics.

Our activism broadened from protesting the rights of individuals—women did have a right to choose to have an abortion as supported by several US Supreme Court rulings—to educating the broader public through protests and our continued presence. It became easier to defend the clinics and women's individual healthcare choices with the volunteers we had. Our patient protectors were needed less frequently due to additional court rulings against anti-choice protesters, arrests of some of their leaders, and their focus on efforts in other cities around the state and country.

Several years later, after much of the public outcry over abortion had subsided, I was called to a clinic downtown for assistance. There was no time for the phone tree. With permission, I left work and went to the clinic in downtown Grand Rapids near the YMCA and found a handful of anti-choice protesters standing at the steps of the clinic. The steps began right at the sidewalk so they were within their legal rights to stand on public property and protest. Yet, I was there to uphold the rights of women to pursue their own healthcare choice. I grabbed a pro-choice sign, donned my pro-choice shirt, and proceeded to assist patients into the clinic.

In between patients, I talked with the few anti-choice protesters. One of these older protesting women said her daughter was in the clinic. When asked why, she said she was having an abortion. Something hypocritical here, I thought, when someone would bring their daughter to have an abortion and then protest outside against the procedure. One of many memories I will never forget.

We always thought Grand Rapids was a target nationally because of its dominant religions and conservative philosophy. As the protests and actions on both sides increased, we realized that it was a national situation with Grand Rapids just being part of it. When the activities declined, much of the anti-choice effort ended up in more conservative states like Missouri and Kansas.

PCA continued to thrive, but got smaller as activism at its peak was no longer needed. We did continue the education part through speaking events and marches. This too declined until the early 2000s when I moved to Arizona. My understanding is that the organization soon after was disbanded.

Our legacy is rooted in a woman's right to choose, of which countless women appreciated our efforts and the public began to shift to a more pro-choice position. We always referred to the 20 percent of people to the far left and 20 percent to the far right. The 60 percent was referred to as the "mushy middle." This was the group that we were targeting our efforts and where we made most of our inroads.

The Young Lords' Legacy: From Puerto Rico to Chicago to Grand Rapids

by José "Cha-Cha" Jimenez

Organizing Latinos to support the successful Chicago mayoral campaign of Harold Washington took a toll on me personally, including divorce and homelessness. To stay in Chicago meant embarrassing the mayor and possibly derailing our accomplishments. There were also daily death threats from several bitter sources, including local gangs, police, and the mafia-connected Streets and Sanitation Department. My plan was to get away briefly, but I ended up in Grand Rapids, Michigan, in a homeless shelter on Division Street's skid row. Here—in Grand Rapids—is when I started college, first at Grand Rapids Community College and later at Grand Valley State University; married twice; and, eventually re-committed myself to the Young Lords with more fervor than when I began.[1]

To fully comprehend the legacy of a movement, you must first understand the political, economic, and social forces that created it. The Young Lords Movement was formally launched on September 23, 1968, in Chicago, Illinois. But the roots of this movement go far deeper, reaching back to European and American imperialist policies of the nineteenth century.[2] As most Puerto Ricans know, September 23, 1868, marks a critical national anniversary: the first time the nation rose up militarily to demand independence from Spanish rule. The Puerto Rican struggle for independence continued as the island was subjected to further foreign rule, including US occupation in 1898 and well into the twenty-first century.[3]

From Puerto Rico to Chicago

Decades of economic underdevelopment and US government-sponsored programs, like Operation Bootstrap, which destroyed agrarian farms to make way for manufacturing, propelled hundreds of thousands of Puerto Ricans from the island to the US mainland through the 1940s and 1950s.[4] Initially working for the war effort in steel mills and in agriculture and domestic service, many of these young Puerto Rican men and women found their way to cities, settling in Boston, Philadelphia, Newark, New York, Chicago, and Milwaukee, among others. These Puerto Rican migrants left a lasting mark where they settled. It was the children of these migrants who launched the Young Lords Movement.

Rather than finding places of opportunity, Puerto Ricans in the 1940s and 1950s in cities across the US faced discrimination in housing, jobs, and even at church. The first Puerto Rican immigrants to the Midwest, and Chicago specifically, had opened up Northside Catholic sanctuaries to Spanish mass,[5] but these Spanish masses were relegated to basements and adjacent church halls. White ethnics did not want Latinos in the main chapels.

Violence and the threat of violence was rampant. In 1956, the Dragons gang—the largest gang in New York City, where 90 percent of Puerto Rico's diaspora lived—traveled to Chicago by car loads to aid in a major, week-long street battle that broke out at a neighborhood carnival in Lincoln Park at St. Michael's Catholic Church. The New York City gang was outraged that a couple of Puerto Rican churchwomen had been beaten and raped by a Chicago-based white ethnic gang.

Without support from police, schools, or other official channels, young Puerto Ricans were left to defend themselves and their communities in this physical, violent way.

Yet, the Young Lords and other Latino youth groups not only used violence against violence, they organized the Puerto Rican community; they helped open-up candy stores, pizzerias, and the park and beach areas that excluded Puerto Rican families. Latino barrios began to emerge within Chicago's neighborhoods, like Lincoln Park, Wicker Park, Uptown, Humboldt Park, Pilsen, Lakeview, Downtown La Clark, and La Madison. Small businesses, social clubs, softball teams, parades, and neighborhood organizations took hold.

This Latino power frightened white ethnics. This was especially true when it came to who controlled the prime real estate situated near the park, Lake Michigan, and next to the downtown Loop. Just as the Latino community was growing, Mayor Richard J. Daley intervened by "cleansing the blight," displacing these primarily minority communities, and creating an all-white upper-class "suburb within the city."[6] Mayor Daley sought to overturn "white flight" and bring back the lost tax dollars of whites that had fled Chicago for the suburbs when African Americans, Latinos, and poor whites migrated into the inner city.[7] The mechanism for bringing the city's white population back: urban renewal. Though urban renewal was camouflaged as city redevelopment, it was basically a racist and corrupt master plan to maintain old-school segregation by pushing out minorities and the poor to the suburbs and bringing the suburbs into Chicago. In Chicago, the plan was co-devised by former Hamburg gang leader, Richard J. Daley's, corrupt political friends—friends like Tom Keane, Dan Rostenkowski, and Fast Eddie Vrdolyak, who all ended up in prison.

To young Latinos, including myself, the larger plan was clear. The signs that read "Old Town" on storefronts sent a message to those of us living in these neighborhoods that the political machine—the bankers, the developers, and the neighborhood associations—were going to rip off prime real estate from our families, thereby destroying our neighborhood power. We compared it to colonialism and the diminution of power in Puerto Rico.

Mayor Richard J. Daley became the clear enemy. It was his fifty-year master plan, after all. He was the mayor when these low income and Latino neighborhoods were rehabbed or bulldozed, when people were evicted from their homes.

In the winter of 1960, after more than a decade of social, political, and economic discrimination and violence, Orlando Davila called seven of us together to form a street gang to defend ourselves from the beatings of the other white ethnic gangs. In 1964, I was voted in and became the president; and in 1968, I re-organized several branches of the gang, including the women auxiliaries called Young

Lordettes, into a civil and human rights group called the Young Lords Organization; in New York, Young Lords Party, and today just Young Lords. We organized beyond the former gang, working with schools and the broader community. Today classes on the Young Lords are being taught in universities and our history is a part of most Latino Studies curricula.

The Young Lords have stood for unity and have always come to the aid of friends in the movement. We stood for the freedom fighter, Oscar Lopez Rivera, because an attack on one is an attack on all. You cannot fight a battle without a distinction between friends and enemies.

In Chicago, Mayor Daley was the enemy and our friends were all who opposed him and his policies. Coalitions among activist groups and community organizations emerged, like the Rainbow Coalition (Black Panthers, Young Patriots, and Young Lords) and the North Side Cooperative Ministry of Rev. Bruce and Eugenia Ransier Johnson of the United Methodist Church (UMC).

The risks for our activism and coalition building were high: UMC Rev. Bruce Johnson, his wife Eugenia, and the assistant UMC Rev. Sergio Herrera of the Young Lords People's Church were all murdered, bludgeoned to death for their support of Latinos and the poor of Lincoln Park. At the time they were killed, the People's Church was being fined $200 a day for allowing a Young Lords' free community day care center in their gym.

At the time of the People's Church murders, I was in jail with another felony, adding to seventeen other felonies. Fred Hampton of the Black Panthers, who had nine felonies, was targeted and killed two months later. Our entire Young Lords' Central Committee eventually had to go underground. We set up a training school in Tomah, Wisconsin, until I returned to Chicago to do a year in prison, fight the other charges against me, and eventually run for alderman of the Forty-sixth Ward in 1975. We didn't win, but we received 39 percent of the vote, falling shy of the 51 percent needed to win.

Our primary mission was to unite our divided Puerto Rican nation, which today is comprised of four million people living in

Puerto Rico and four million residing inside the US. The Young Lords' mission, though it emerged out of a local need, resonated across the country. We grew, building a strong organization and a movement throughout Latino barrios nationwide. We organized neighborhoods and communities throughout the country, broadening our base of support. We adopted a range of teaching tools to empower Latino barrios and promote self-determination. We organized: door-to-door community organizing campaigns, as well as newspapers and outreach programs modeled after the Black Panthers.

A clear distinction between cadre work and people work prevented us from becoming sectarian and helped to build a more democratic, collective People's Struggle. Repression might have murdered the Johnsons, Mark Clark, and Chairman Fred Hampton but it will never kill our movement. The Young Lords viewed themselves humbly as part of a continuous struggle for change.

From Chicago to Grand Rapids

I landed in Grand Rapids in 1986.

It did not take long for me to see that poverty, segregation, and discrimination in Grand Rapids were all too familiar. Similar to earlier development efforts under colonialism in Puerto Rico and urban renewal in Chicago, Grand Rapids, Michigan, is currently experiencing a "comeback" on the backs of the city's poor.

Much like Lincoln Park in Chicago, throughout the seventies and eighties, I witnessed Grand Rapids's city hall encourage neighborhood blight by providing minimal police safety, insufficient building inspections, or other city services to poor areas of the city.

To me, it was similar to Chicago: a land grab sponsored by city hall. Neighborhood residents pushed out to make way for breweries and condominiums.

In an effort to "improve" the area for Grand Valley State University students and develop student housing, the city moved the low-income, minority residents out. In the process of redevelopment, city blocks were left vacant, ostensibly to force homeowners from surrounding properties to sell cheap to housing conglomerates like Rockford Construction, fearing their loss of property value. The city used building inspectors, realtors, neighborhood associations, and various other methods to take the land.

The city's planners and elected officials envisioned Grand Rapids as an Athens, a Paris, or a Buenos Aires. The city has created parks and "walkable communities." The city's art scene is thriving. The city is now known nationally for ArtPrize and beer.

Grand Rapids is having a "comeback" for the rich, not the poor. The new medical mile, the new parks, the new bicycle paths, and the new salmon fishing and kayaking sports capital of the world is not for the city's poor and minority residents.

Grand Rapids-Chicago- Puerto Rico, it is all the same. Politicians and city officials claim inclusivity, pointing to the token Black and Latino names on their letterheads or housing board and committee meetings, but minorities are given little voice or power in devising plans.

The Young Lords' legacy lives on, in part, through my continued commitment to building unity among marginalized minorities, eliminating racist segregation, and ensuring the interests of minorities and the poor throughout the city and the region. Today, my activism looks different than it did when I lived in Chicago—when I was the president of the Young Lords— but my mission remains the same.

Development should be controlled by neighborhood residents, not by the neighborhood associations of absentee landlords and developers, nor the elites from downtown. Cities belong to all the people.

---

1. For more information, see DePaul University's Young Lord Newspaper Collection, http://digicol.lib.depaul.edu/cdm/landingpage/collection/younglords, and the Grand Valley State University Oral History Project at www.gvsu.edu/younglords.

2. Marisabel Bras, M. *The Changing of the Guard: Puerto Rico in 1898* (Hispanic Division Library of Congress, 2014), http://loc.gov/rr/hispanic/1898/bras.html.

3. José L. Vázquez Calzada, *La población de Puerto Rico y su trayectoria histórica* (Río Piedras, P.R.: Escuela Graduada de Salud Pública, Recinto de Ciencias Médicas, Universidad de Puerto Rico, 1988), p. 286; data for 1970-1990 are from Francisco L. Rivera Batiz and Carlos Santiago, *Island Paradox: Puerto Rico in the 1990s* (New York: Russell Sage Foundation, 1996), http://lcw.lehman/depts/latinampuertorican/latinoweb/Puerto Rico/1950.html.

4. Melanie Shell-Weiss, *Coming to Miami: A Social History* (Gainesville, FL: University Press of Florida, 2009).

5. Headley, D. J. Oral history video interview (2012). GVSU: Special Collections. http://www.gvsu.edu/younglords.

6. Andrew H. Malcolm, "Chicago's loop is coming back alive, even if it hasn't gone full circle yet," *New York Times* (New York), February 1, 1983.

7. Greg Hinz & Steven R. Strahler, "Mayor Daley runs up big debts building his global city; what about the rest of Chicago?" *Crain's Chicago Business.* (Chicago, IL), June 12, 2010.

An earlier version of this piece was previously published in CT Latino News.

Shaping The Narrative

...where we identify the issues facing us now

I Fall on Gold Ave.

by Fable the Poet

November on Gold Avenue

Blocks away from *The Bitter End*
of a neighborhood divided.
The city doesn't even try to hide it.

But,
They keep trying to test me.

The Little Caesars round the corner
Says: "We no longer serve Pepperoni Cheese Bread"
As if they stopped stocking
Pepperoni...
Or Cheese Bread...

I'm not going to lie ya'll,

This might be the straw that broke the camel's pack,
But I smoke American Spirit,
A pack a day keeping the stress of rent raising away.

They are charging Market rate,
Without a market in sight.

We don't need a Meijer,
Or Target down the street.
We are wearing bullseyes already.

They are gunning for our exit—
Drive by
But not at night,
There are NO street lights.
You won't be able to witness.

Bask in that for a while.

My neighbor tells me
The woman that used to live here,
had "one hell of a green thumb."

The roses she planted before her eviction,
Tell me "good morning" from my shady porch.

They wave hello,
Tip their crimson fall floppy hat at me through gravel stones
showing me she WAS one hell of a botanist.

Too bad passion didn't pay the bills.

I wonder if he will tell the next tenants.
That I was "one hell of a writer"

I wonder if the words of encouragement
That me and my girlfriend
litter on their children's minds,
will last longer than the value of our home.

Longer than the stories of jade digits

The ghost of tenants past still haunts our entryway.

I wonder if our landlord will paint
over the hieroglyphics left by HER children,
Or if they will stay as a reminder that we are only as good as the green
In our pockets,
Not the crayon coated phrase that greets you
when entering out home.

The voice of this pre-pubescent child bellows
Pipe organ—and brings me to church every time I go to leave.

I imagine Fingers still embracing Crayola keys
It reads...
"A**hole".

I assume this message was written to the people
that asked them to go,
those "remodeling" their home,
The same way they are restructuring the community,
For higher income.

It is November on Gold Street.

In July,
There was a ranch home behind us.

There is now a concrete slab.
Where a home once stood,
Yet here,
I hear,
We have an issue with lack of housing...
Irony.

Two doors down from me
a shiny new blue door
secures the nicest residence on the street.

A home erected quicker than my morals.

Every Friday night when they party,
I can hear it from down the street.
Wonder if the kids in ten of the homes around us
are able to sleep.

I imagine stealing their big screen TV.
I can see it every time when I walk by
Simultaneously pacing and contemplating if I should
ask them to "PLEASE quiet down."

I imagine how good surround that I can't afford,
would sound with that PHAT screen in my living room.

I wonder if it would tune out their music,
Or the ghost of tenants past,
Or the sound of police stopping the residents they are busy
blaming for the theft.

Ya know, the brown ones
Who will "Match the description."

It's November on Gold Avenue
and I just want to focus on the leaves.

But I already know they want us to
Leave.

Until then—I will play with the children while they are still
here.

I will create a symphony of laughter that rattles windows
awaking college students from hangover coated slumbers.

I will make them wish we would quiet down.
I will show the neighbors that we don't have to be quiet,
That we shouldn't be.

The influence for this poem, and a few others like it is simple: our city is changing.

When a city grows around those existing around it, it is an incredible thing to witness.

When a city grows, then people can no longer afford homes in the neighborhoods they love, have always lived in, and no longer feel welcome to—that is when you have an issue.

We have multiple issues here, and one side effect is displacement.

The illness is gentrification.

Stopping the War on Women in Conservative Grand Rapids

by Charlsie Dewey

For me, STOP WOW (Stop the War on Women) was one of my first forays into grassroots activism. I'd never really understood the power of grassroots organizing or how I could fit in.

In college, as friends gathered regularly to protest the Iraq War, I belittled their efforts as a waste of time, but later, when I was living in Chicago, I began to see the power of activism. As a journalist for the *Windy City Times*, I covered a handful of protests and vigils and other grassroots efforts to raise awareness around a slew of issues and I began to feel a tug of wanting to join these efforts.

Coming back to Grand Rapids, a well-known conservative bastion, I felt isolated from like-minded people until one afternoon, walking through the Eastown Street Fair, I was stopped by a woman decades older than me who asked a very simple question, "Would you like to see more women in political office?"

Of course I did and before I knew it, I was attending my first meeting of the Progressive Women's Alliance of West Michigan (PWA), which put on educational programs around political issues on a nearly monthly basis. The women of PWA welcomed me and I quickly joined the organization's program committee, helping draft press releases and other materials advertising upcoming speakers and events. It was a crash course in local and state politics and it was exciting.

When the idea for STOP WOW began to emerge, I was eager to be involved. I'd become an activist.

On May 24, 2012, nearly 500 women, men, and children gathered at Rosa Parks Circle in downtown Grand Rapids to stand up for the right of every woman to make her own choices regarding her body.

It was believed to be the largest gathering of individuals around a progressive issue in decades in the city and it was the result of a small group of women who, just two months earlier, had gotten angry enough to hatch a plan for a rally and had worked doggedly to bring that plan to fruition over the next nine weeks.

That year and the year prior had seen the introduction of hundreds of legislative bills across the country—including in Michigan—aimed at reducing or eliminating women's reproductive rights. In Michigan alone, there were fourteen anti-choice bills under consideration at that time. Those bills included efforts to defund Planned Parenthood in the state, to require fetal remains to be disposed of in the same manner as a human body, to institute a health insurance ban on abortion coverage, and to pass a personhood bill that would in effect outlaw abortion and ban birth control methods.

The erosion of *Roe v. Wade* had been taking place for decades, but in 2011 and 2012, efforts were being made with a renewed vigor and maliciousness and the phrase, "war on women," was gaining prominence and widespread attention as women began to feel they were truly under attack by their state and federal representatives—the women behind STOP WOW among them.

So on an early spring day, with snow still clinging to the ground, nearly a dozen women met at a local restaurant at lunchtime to begin plans for a rally they hoped would lead to greater political engagement and more voters at the polls in November. The group included Bette Sebastian, Ruth Kelly, Susan Lewis, Noreen Myers, Mary Alice Williams, Jo Ellyn Clarey, Ellyn Wolfson, Dani Vilella, Tansy Harris, Angela Miske, and myself.

Most of its members were seasoned activists and original founders or members of the political action committee Progressive Women's Alliance of West Michigan (PWA), which had formed in 2003 to enhance the voices of the region's progressives and raise money for progressive candidates. Along with supporting a slew of candidates for office, several members of the group had also previously carried out a successful billboard campaign with PWA, highlighting the Michigan Supreme Court's ranking in 2008 as the "worst in the nation." These women knew how to organize, how to fundraise, and how to get things done.

In those initial meetings, the group chose a name, STOP WOW, which stood for Stop the War on Women, and a logo, designed by Miske, which included the image of Rosie the Riveter popping out from within the "O" in WOW and carrying a protest sign reading "STOP." Both were selected because of their cultural significance and easily identifiable messaging.

The group also clarified its mission statement and key messaging, which read, "STOP WOW is a coalition of women and organizations who promote reproductive justice and are committed to protecting women's choices. We are *pro-choices*, meaning that we are focused on several aspects of women's reproductive health and liberties: contraception, fertility treatments and options, emergency contraception, marriage, parenthood. We believe in the Constitutional right to privacy, the dignity of every human being, the significance of reason and the basic equality of all individuals."

Over those initial weeks, the group also grew to nearly fifteen members, all of whom squeezed around local restaurant tables week after week as the planning progressed.

Locally-based entertainment producer Teresa Thome was recruited to produce the rally. STOP WOW also gained a cohort of like-minded organizations eager to add their names to the rally as co-sponsors: Progressive Women's Alliance of West Michigan, ACLU of Michigan, National Organization of Women Greater Grand Rapids Chapter, Planned Parenthood Advocates of Michigan, and Grand Valley State University Women's Center. The rally began to draw media attention with a handful of local journalists interviewing STOP WOW members ahead of the event.

Some weeks it felt like time was moving too fast and everything couldn't possibly come together by the May 24 rally deadline and yet, the members of Stop WOW persevered. Over twenty local speakers, entertainers and activists volunteered to participate in the rally, filling out the two-hour program schedule. There was always a fear—"What if no one shows up?" or "What if the turnout is so measly it's embarrassing?" To quell that fear, efforts were made to attract the attention of MSNBC's Rachel Maddow—to no avail.

It turned out Grand Rapids didn't need a celebrity headliner to show up, however. On May 24, as it grew closer to 6:00 P.M., people began trickling in from all directions and filling Rosa Parks Circle.

First there were 100, then 200, then 300, and they kept coming.

People of every age poured in, some with their own hand-made signs, some eagerly picking up STOP WOW yard signs that were being handed out at one of the tables set up around the perimeters along with STOP WOW contraception packs re-purposed into mirrored compacts or noisemakers. A group of senior citizens arrived by bus from one of the local retirement communities, recruited by Vernis Schad. They sat in folding chairs with parasols shielding them from the blaring sun.

The mood was one of excitement and determination as Teresa Thome kicked off the evening by welcoming everyone and introducing a brief video of former first lady Betty Ford, who during her lifetime had been a vocal supporter of women's reproductive justice and the Equal Rights Amendment.

By 8:00 P.M., with the words of Mary Alice Williams and Dani Vilella fresh in people's minds, the rally concluded and the crowd dispersed into the Grand Rapids evening. The STOP WOW founders gathered to celebrate at a small bar in the North Monroe neighborhood of downtown. High on the success of the evening, it seemed as if no one wanted to see the night end. Members gathered on the sidewalk outside of the bar and talked for another hour, plans for "what's next" already brewing.

STOP WOW had done what it set out to do—stand up and be heard.

Fresh off its victory with the rally, STOP WOW members gathered in June and began planning a follow up effort, a fall billboard and bus board campaign designed to keep the organization's name in the community and to encourage Grand Rapidians to vote for reproductive justice in November.

On October 10, STOP WOW's message was carried on billboards and buses across the city, and the organization held a kickoff party the following day at the Meanwhile Bar. Again, the campaign grabbed people's attention. Local media responded with interview requests and STOP WOW supporters proudly showed up to support the campaign. STOP WOW signs dotted yards in neighborhoods across the city for months, and even years, after the rally and the billboard campaign had concluded.

STOP WOW eventually disbanded as its members took on roles within other organizations, but the group made its mark—the logo is still recognizable today. PWA and STOP WOW connected me to my city in a way I'd never imagined, and both organizations introduced me to women who still inspire me and who I feel lucky to call friends.

Facing Racism: The Lasting Effects of Discrimination in Grand Rapids's Southeast Community

by Michelle Jokisch Polo

"I love my community, and my community is a very poor community, and it could do so much better if it had greater access," says Alice Johnson, a resident of the Madison Square neighborhood. In 1976, while residing in Arkansas, Johnson made the decision to pack up her bags and move to Grand Rapids. Her husband at the time had managed to get a job in town, and she decided to move in hopes of finding better opportunities for work.

"Coming from Arkansas, this community was predominantly Black and looked very big and pleasant," Johnson explains, referring to the Madison Square neighborhood.

After moving here and separating from her husband, the single mother of three was working tirelessly as a certified nurse at the Grand Rapids Home for Veterans, trying to save up enough money to purchase the home she was renting on 1441 Lafayette Avenue SE.

"I didn't have good credit, and I had three little children, making it very difficult," says Johnson.

According to Johnson, a German family in the area decided to advocate for her with Union Bank and Trust, a local banking institution of the time, and she was able to receive a loan amounting to $3,000, the down payment for the house. Since then, she has been able to provide a secure home environment to all eight of her children, seven of whom she fostered and eventually adopted.

"My children have grown up to be very good in spite of the difficult circumstances we have faced," says Johnson.

There is No Ally-Ship in Colorblindness

Johnson's story is emblematic of thousands of others who left the southern US for Grand Rapids, many of whom moved to the city's southeast communities. In the decades following the Civil

War, Black Americans hoping to escape racist policies and institutions in the southern states and to find more opportunities, from education to careers, moved to the north during the Great Migration in the early twentieth century, including to Grand Rapids. The city's Black community grew from a population of 665 in 1910 to 2,795 in 1930, according to federal statistics. However, once Black Americans arrived in northern cities, including in Grand Rapids, they faced much of the same oppression they experienced in the South. Author and historian Todd Robinson points out in his book, *A City Within a City*, that "Michigan's Jim Crow customs were often disguised in arguments about free enterprise and the freedom of association."

For example, the price of everything from beverages to rent was often far higher for Black Grand Rapidians than their white neighbors. "Even a basic commodity, such as coffee, routinely cost Black customers five times as much: They paid fifty cents, while whites only paid ten cents," writes Robinson.

Nearly 8,000 Black residents moved to the city between 1950 and 1960, according to government statistics, but, as in years prior, almost all of them discovered they were aggressively excluded from most of the city when it came to renting or owning homes: no one would consider renting them housing unless it was in a neighborhood that often had decaying housing stock (such as in the city's southeast). And as far as owning a place? That proved far more difficult than renting, with banks routinely turning down Black residents.

As Black Grand Rapidians were paying more for everything from rent to restaurant meals and were being paid less than their white counterparts at their jobs, they also were being forced to shell out more for housing in "the oldest section of a racially divided city," Robinson writes of the mid-twentieth century.

By the time Johnson moved to the city in the 1970s, things were, little by little, changing, with some Black residents accessing loans and purchasing property. But, as Johnson explains, access to financial opportunities was limited, and continues to be so. To understand the struggles that members of the southeast communities continue to face, it is imperative to take a closer look at the history.

Historical Segregation and Racism in Grand Rapids

It was 1872 when the former mayor of Grand Rapids, Charles Comstock, began recruiting Black residents from Tennessee and Mississippi to come work for his new barrel-making plant, as is detailed in the account, *African Americans in the Furniture City: The Struggle for Civil Rights in Grand Rapids*, by historian and Grand Rapidian Dr. Randal Maurice Jelks. The deal Comstock offered these citizens included housing arrangements, and with this assurance many packed up their belongings and moved into "the Hon. C.C. Comstock's Hotel de Afrique." This apartment complex was built to accommodate up to twenty Black families and later became known as Comstock's Row.

"This was a way of controlling workers and preventing workers from organizing," Jelks says of the tenement building located on what was then North Canal Street and is now Monroe Avenue, near Leonard Street, during an interview with *Rapid Growth*.

It was not only Black citizens who were being recruited to work in these low paying jobs, but Dutch and Polish immigrants also agreed to this type of work. Even though Dutch and Polish families were also experiencing disadvantages, they had no interest in forming alliances with the Black working class.

"Though free from physical bondage, racial segregation surfaced as a tool to minimize competition between African Americans and immigration groups," Jelks says.

As a result, Black people were on their own in the fight against inequitable Jim Crow practices following the Civil War, says Jelks. On the one hand, white elites thought their anti-slavery sentiments and charity toward Black individuals was a sign of ally-ship, yet they continued to exclude Black residents from being a part of the rising manufacturing industry. And the white working class attempted to achieve economic capital at the expense of the Black working class.

As the number of Dutch immigrants began to increase throughout the city of Grand Rapids, Black residents were confronted with the harsh reality that employers preferred to hire these individuals over them. With the increase of negative sentiments, treatment, and false stereotypes of Black Americans came the further separation and segregation between the white working class and Black citizens, as evidenced by the formation in the 1920s of the first Klu Klux Klan "club" in Grand Rapids at South High School, located at Hall Street and Jefferson Avenue. At the time, many poor working-class whites studied alongside Black students. But as the white working and middle class gained economic capital, they took the opportunity to flee south of the railroad tracks, where Black Americans were prohibited from settling until 1970.

By the mid-1950s, many white residents had fled to the suburbs in search of more homogeneous communities, and, as a result of the distance between downtown and the suburbs, found it increasingly difficult to access the city proper. To help address the issue, the former city planning director, Keith Honey, proposed the expansion of US 131 in 1955. The proposal was meant to easily encourage mobility between the suburbs and downtown Grand Rapids, at the expense of physically dividing Black and brown neighborhoods in the city's southeast communities.

"Urban renewal comes to a neighborhood like Madison Square, turning it from a white, middle-class community into an all-Black neighborhood," Jelks says of the neighborhood that faced significant racially-motivated disinvestment after the white residents left.

For affluent white residents, the development of US 131, and later the twelve-mile-long I-96 east to west link, were signs of urban renewal. These developments were later known as the "best urban freeway network in the nation" per Gordon Olson's historical account, *Grand Rapids: A City Renewed*.

But, as Olson later details in his work, the highway development caused the demolition and relocation of more than 1,000 west side families. Despite the displacement, many Grand Rapid-

the development of U.S. 131 and I-96 as a way to advance the industry and increase accessibility to downtown.

"As housing developments, commercial centers, and industrial complexes moved outward from Grand Rapids's core, new roads became essential to the area's economic well-being," explains Olson.

In attempts to revitalize and encourage movement to downtown, city leaders sought to use federal government funds, approved by President Dwight Eisenhower, to provide affordable housing opportunities for low-income families. Initially, 10 percent of these funds were meant to be used on nonresidential projects, but the percentage was later raised to 35 percent. This meant that only 65 percent of the funding would be used to help house families in need, many of whom belonged to the Black working class.

According to US census statistics for 1960, Black Americans in Grand Rapids were living in segregated neighborhoods and working low paying jobs. These residents were not only bound by their lack of economic capital, but they also faced physical boundaries, as they were prohibited from purchasing homes outside of Hall Street on the south, Cherry Street on the north, Fuller on the east, and the river to the west.

Today, the southeast neighborhoods still hold the city's greatest concentration of Black residents, with 51 percent of Grand Rapids's Black population residing within the boundaries of Wealthy Street, Cottage Grove, US 131 and Madison Square, per 2013 US census data obtained from the Dorothy A. Johnson Center for Philanthropy at Grand Valley State University.

The second largest demographic of the area are Latinx residents, who make up 27 percent of the area's overall population. White residents constitute 17 percent. When comparing these numbers to neighborhoods mere blocks away, like the more affluent East Hills and Heritage Hill area, the numbers of Black residents in these neighborhoods significantly decrease. In the East Hills and Heritage Hill area, Black residents make up 14 percent of the community, while whites represent 72 percent of all residents.

"To talk about racial reconciliation, you are talking about economics and structures. Without having a means of gaining capital access—you keep people locked down. And those keeping people locked down are all 'well-meaning' people," Jelks says.

Looking Ahead: Attaining a Sustainable Community

Today residents of the Madison Square neighborhood continue to experience a lack of access to economic capital, education, housing stability, and a healthy home environment. In spite of these factors, residents of this community are working together with advocates from organizations like Seeds of Promise and LincUp to gain access to spaces of influence and to help foster self-sustainable neighborhoods.

"Our work is informed primarily through our community's neighbors, and through strategic organizing and empowerment we are creating our own platforms to make change," explains Ronald Jimmerson, Sr., executive director and co-founder of Seeds of Promise.

For Johnson, believing in the power of her community means she is willing to call out a history of oppression and deep-seated problems she and her neighbors face living in the Madison Square neighborhood.

"I don't have access to a whole lot of things in our community. We have to go outside of our community to obtain them," Johnson says of the lack of affordable grocery shops, clothing stores, and pharmacies in the neighborhood.

Looking to the future, Johnson hopes her advocacy encourages others to invest their economic capital into the southeast communities.

"We have some really good people who could do so much good if they had easily available resources," Johnson says.

An earlier version of this piece was published at Rapid Growth Media.

Leading a New Latina Narrative

by Mindy Ysasi

This piece was written in consultation with: Allison Lugo-Knapp, co-founder Latina Network of West Michigan; Rebeca Velazquez-Publes, co-founder Latina Network of West Michigan; and Stacy Stout, co-founder Latina Network of West Michigan

"Preservation of one's own culture does not require contempt or disrespect for other cultures."

-César E. Chávez.

The above quote from César E. Chávez offers a framework for how and why we built, from the ground-up, a network for Latinas in West Michigan. In the fall of 2014, four women came together to start what is now known as the Latina Network of West Michigan.

When Allison, Beca, Stacy, and I first met, we were unsure what we were building, but we knew we wanted to stay true to our values. First, we wanted whatever we built to be focused on the people of the group, not the four of us. Our goal was a movement of women that was both organic and collective. Second, we recognized the strength of creating awareness that Latinas are not monolithic. The four founders represented Latinas that had much in common, but also had very different experiences: some spoke Spanish, but not all; some were from West Michigan; and we all had different careers.

We wanted to create a space that was specifically *for* Latinas. This desire was manifest in our interest in ensuring our growth as Latina leaders, as well as in fostering racial healing.

***

When I went to Grand Valley in 2003, I thought it was the most diverse place I had ever been and then found out it was a predominately white institution. Growing up in Grand Rapids and attending Catholic Central, I did not have many Latino friends in school. Today Latinos represent 16 percent of the population of Grand Rapids and are the largest group of people of color in our city. But our city is still a tale of two cities: one where people of color often experience racialized outcomes in income and employment, in educational attainment, and in wealth.

The growth of Grand Rapids has been rapid, but not always inclusive. In a city that is not too big, many jobs are still filled via who you know, how you are perceived, and where you went to school. In Grand Rapids, relationships can be powerful. The Latina Network is especially relevant given this context; there are many instances of women who have the talent and experience, but are not always able to find opportunity in Grand Rapids. They lack the network.

Too often the four of us were asked to be on boards, to offer names of Latinas to apply for jobs, and to generally serve as the spokespeople for a large community in our city and county. The network was born out of our belief that there was not a pipeline issue in regards to Latina leadership in our community; rather, we needed to highlight the women in our community and ensure connections.

My co-founders and I met many times prior to the first meeting. We shared our experiences as women of color in Grand Rapids, thoughts of the stories of our sisters, and recounted the pain of not belonging. We believed that an opportunity to feel like we *belonged*, rather than be others, would be a driver for more inclusive opportunities for Latinas.

We connected with our friends to negotiate free space; we are indebted to Franco Silva, who was at Amway, and who secured GRid70 for our first meeting. We talked to fellow board members, mom groups, leadership development program participants, and alumni we knew from Grand Valley State University. We intentionally reached out to people personally and let them know to bring their children, reducing the barrier of not having childcare. We bet on the fact that other Latinas had similar experiences to ours: wanting to belong and be engaged, but not as the token Latina.

***

Over forty women signed up for that first event. During our first meeting we asked questions to help us drive the future of the organization:

What does Latina leadership look like in our community?

What do you, as a Latina leader, need for continued and future success?

We asked what happens after this meeting and many expressed their desire to connect on a more regular basis. From that first meeting, we planned out the next six months of events and asked other women to be part of a leadership team to ensure the leadership went beyond the four founders.

Today, we host monthly events, partner with other organizations to support their work, host social lunch meetings, and engage in civic engagement activities. Last year we engaged in a voter registration drive, which was a part of the Movies in the Park event. While we want our own space to connect and learn, we also want to be a part of the multiple events in Grand Rapids. We have also partnered with leadership programs focused on getting more women to run for office and to begin attending our city commission meetings.

We have around fifty women who attend our monthly events and over 300 women on our main social media network. Connecting and building a community goes beyond our monthly events, and includes a book club and one-on-one meet-ups. Out of our book club we found out that many of our members felt like they were faking their financial security, so we will offer a full financial series in the fall of 2017.

As founders, we see success in other women taking on leadership roles, exploring their own identities, and actively supporting each other in education and employment opportunities. The leadership team meets regularly to set direction and events but we also want to allow for organic spaces of connections; we never want to be prescriptive to how community is created.

While our work is focused on Latinas, we also partner with other women of color in our community to ensure power building and support. Most recently, we held a co-session with Black Women Connect in Grand Rapids. The session was set to build our professional development around crucial conversations. The group left feeling supported after sharing stories of rejection as women of color in the workplace.

Many times people of color are the only people like them in a meeting or even an organization. This can lead to feelings of isolation and stress. We know many women of color that have left Grand Rapids because they felt they did not belong. We want to retain women of color in our city as well as ensure they move into higher-level positions.

People remember how you made them feel, not what you did for them. Our hope is that the Latinas of West Michigan continue to feel the power they have stepped into, that they are valued and necessary to the success of our community.

Our Children Should Not Be Used as Lead Detectors
by Alex Markham

Lead is a neurotoxin, meaning it attacks the brain and nervous system. This is particularly harmful in young children whose systems are at an important stage of development. A child absorbs approximately 40 percent of the lead they come into contact with; this is four to five times the rate of absorption for an adult. For a developing child, the body recognizes lead as a necessary nutrient as it is molecularly similar to iron, so the absorption rate is much higher. Lead can also cross the placenta from mother to baby.

With 188 children testing positive for lead poisoning in 2015, the southeast side of Grand Rapids, specifically zip code 49507, had more children testing positive than anywhere else in the state of Michigan. In fact, three zip codes in Grand Rapids rank in the top ten for child lead poisoning, including 49504, with ninety-six reported cases, and 49503 with ninety-five cases. In the same year, Flint had 111 children test positive in zip codes 48501-48507. The Center for Disease Control (CDC) recommends that children are tested for lead at ages one and two, and before the age of six. Currently, Michigan's testing rate is 20 percent, which is to say, we are only aware of 20 percent of the problem.

Lead is found primarily in three places: paint, soil, and water. In 1978, the federal government banned the use of lead paint. Like many old "rust belt" cities, 81 percent (65,127) of homes in Grand Rapids were built before 1978. In 1975, the use of leaded gasoline began to be phased out, although this took twenty plus years. A trucking route, with trucks spewing leaded gasoline, ran through the areas of the city we now see most affected.

While Grand Rapids has a higher number of homes affected, this situation is not solely ours. 66 percent (3,011,618) of homes in Michigan were built before 1978 compared to 56 percent (74,433,763) nationwide. Lead poisoning is an epidemic across our nation, and while we are united in the same health concern, the specific situation of each community is unique.

The information that Grand Rapids has a large lead problem is not usually well received, whether at a home visit explaining why a child's screening could have come back high, at a community event providing education on services, or just in conversation with friends. The reactions are usually the same: anger and disbelief. "How do we not know?" The answer is simple: Grand Rapids didn't have a crisis. There was no sudden change, no catalyst, no national outcry.

The Response

Get the Lead Out!, which started in West Michigan in 2004, is a program designed to provide funds for lead abatement with the ultimate goal of making our community safer for children— one home at a time. Get the Lead Out! currently aims to address lead in fifty homes per year. Left to this resource alone, it would take 1,302 years to make every home in Grand Rapids safe. We needed a better solution. The education and resources provided by Healthy Homes were desperately needed in our community.

Healthy Homes Coalition of West Michigan is the result of a collaborative effort by local organizations that joined with parents with children affected by lead poisoning who took action after recognizing that, to thoroughly address the lead problem in Grand Rapids, we'd need a permanent organization to provide a wider array of services. Healthy Homes is taking the lessons learned from childhood lead poisoning prevention and applying them to a wider array of healthy housing issues for children.

Strengthening the Fight at Home

Lead poisoning is a complicated issue, tied to poverty, race, housing crises, discrimination, and more. Even with the resources and dedication of Healthy Homes, truly solving the lead problem in Grand Rapids requires the efforts of multiple organizations that have expertise on a multitude of issues. In Grand Rapids, this took the form of a coalition of organizations and people affected by lead combining their efforts in order to make lead abatement a priority for local elected officials.

In response to the rate of lead poisonings rising in West Michigan for the first time in a decade, a town hall meeting was hosted in March 2016 as a collaborative effort between Healthy Homes, the Grand Rapids Urban League, LINC, and the NAACP. It was there that our legislators, community leaders, residents, and others listened to the multitude of lead-related concerns, discussed what was being done for the residents of Flint, and pledged to address lead in our city. Community members wanted greater access to education, more extensive outreach, and services to be provided before children became sick. From this, the Healthy Homes Peer Education Program was started in April 2016 and I was given the opportunity to partner with them to create it.

My Journey to Lead Activism

My experiences in the year leading up to starting the Peer Education program seemed scattered and inconsistent at the time, but were preparing me for something very specific. Within a year, I was volunteering in Detroit, and then Grand Rapids, and then Flint, and then Grand Rapids again.

In August 2014, floods hit many areas of Detroit. Many homes had dangerous mold growing in the basement, causing the household members to become sick. I volunteered with All Hands Volunteers, a disaster response organization, working home-by-home to remove everything down to the cement walls, to remove the mold and rebuild, restoring the home to its previous state. I had no experience in disaster response, I couldn't fix anything on a house, but I learned. Some days I spent rebuilding, feeling strong and invincible. Others I spent helping homeowners sort through their belongings, saying goodbye to objects from family or friends that had passed. Sometimes I shared their tears, knowing if I were in their place, I'm not sure I'd be able to let these things go.

I went to Detroit to volunteer my time for what was supposed to be a six-day break from nursing school. The need was so great that the project ended up being extended, month by month, for seven more months. Despite the fact that my mother thought I was having some kind of crisis, I decided to stay with the project, which meant dropping out of nursing school and cancelling a mortgage application to buy my first house in order to continue to do this work.

This was the most empowering and emotionally draining experience of my life, and once that kind of connection to community happens there's no going back. As I prepared to say goodbye to this experience that had such an impact on my life, I knew I'd need to find a way to continue this work closer to home.

Five years prior, I had done lead testing for a clinic that often referred families to Healthy Homes, so when I was looking for volunteer opportunities in my own community, volunteering at Healthy Homes seemed like an appropriate place to start. I worked first with their FEMA program, installing smoke and carbon monoxide detectors and teaching fire safety. During this time, the Flint water crisis was unfolding. Each week, new and horrifying information was coming out about the devastation that lead was causing in Flint. I wanted to use my volunteer time to specifically address lead issues, but I didn't know how I could be involved. Then, during a training to prepare for the Lead Education Day hosted by the Michigan Alliance for Lead Safe Homes, I heard the phrase that felt like a punch to the gut: "Our children should not be used as lead detectors."

Not only did I find my catalyst that day, I also learned a new way to create change. Lead Education Day brings people from all over the state to Lansing to educate elected officials on issues surrounding problems with lead. I was so apprehensive when I first walked down the elaborate hallways of our beautiful state capitol building and into the offices of the people who decide the direction of our state, but I learned something very important that day: you know what happens in your community, your voice matters, and you elected them so they have to listen.

With the determination and sense of widespread community gained from Lead Education Day, I researched how to volunteer to help in the continually developing Flint water crisis. I joined the Genesee County Health Department doing lead education in March 2016 for two clinics. I went in eager to listen and teach, but what I found was a mess. While coalition work is important to tackling complex issues, Flint is an example of cooperation gone wrong. With dozens of organizations, individuals, and companies trying to tackle this issue, everyone was working at cross-purposes and the people influenced by the crisis were not getting the resources or information that they needed. People who had been tested for lead were shocked to find out that, while their tests were negative, the lead had moved from their blood into their bones. While bottled water was being distributed, people were still living as if in a disaster area with cases piling up in the corners of homes. People who had invested everything in their property were finding out that their investment was now worthless. The most common thing that I heard, when I asked people what I could do for them was, "Can you give me my home value back?"

The work in Flint was transitioning and my volunteer time was coming to an end. I had learned too much to let this issue rest. We needed to do better. As the legislators I had just met at Lead Education Day continued to debate and draft and pitch solutions, the crisis continued with real consequences far away from the people controlling the decisions.

Peer Education

One afternoon, shortly after I returned to my volunteer role at Healthy Homes, Paul Haan, the director, came up to ask how things were going. He wanted to know about my recent experiences in Flint and asked if I'd be interested in doing a lead education program in Grand Rapids. I was thrilled, which slightly masked the feeling of unrelenting defeat I still carried after Flint. There was nothing more I could do there, but I'd been given an opportunity to do something here.

The Peer Education Program was created to fill the gap in services between prevention and the period when a child becomes sick enough to warrant the more in-depth programs (these are grant-funded and, therefore, typically more restrictive). To ensure the program is truly accessible, it is free with no income requirements. The only requirement is that a child is in the home twenty hours per week. This hourly requirement allows for services to be extended to caregivers who are often family members.

The Peer Education Program is made up of members of the community, most often people who have experience doing advocacy work in other areas, who volunteer their time to go into the homes of people who are at risk for, or concerned about, lead exposure. At a home visit, we address fire safety, asthma triggers, and lead safety, including a walk-through to look for sources of other health hazards, and can include tests for radon or lead dust. Our educational material comes from Healthy Homes, and a FEMA grant supplies the smoke and carbon monoxide detectors that we provide to families.

As each family and home situation is unique, peer educators often return to the Healthy Homes office with questions for the staff and send along additional resources that are tailored to meet each family's needs. Because of this, our training and program's focus continues to grow and we have added services that include how to test soil, water, pipes, and air ducts for lead, how to apply for the city's home restoration program, and how to report code compliance issues.

To walk into a home, and to be accepted as a stranger, is a humbling experience. We spend one to two hours together and during this time, not only do we address housing hazards, but we often share stories about family, worries as parents, and struggles as single mothers. We leave, hoping that this time has made them safer.

There are also the unexpected lessons. At one home visit, as we walked around and as I inspected the smoke detectors, I reached the upstairs hall, a small landing that had just enough space for my step stool. With little space, it seemed best to place the stool directly under the detector. I twisted off the detector and was greeted by a shower of dead cockroaches. I learned two important things that day.

One: don't ever stand directly under your work area.

Two: when inspecting a new living space, check the date of the smoke detectors, which should have a ten-year lithium battery sealed inside (please none of this, "I burned the toast and so now I'll just remove the batteries" nonsense) and look for brown smudges on the detector or wall behind it. If you see these marks, know that's cockroach excrement and you should ask if the problem has been remedied.

The Peer Education Program is a unique attempt at solving a complicated problem. Healthy Homes, as an established nonprofit organization, works with larger organizations, such as the Federal Emergency Management Agency (FEMA), and federal programs, such as Women Infant and Children (WIC), but gets 49 percent of its funding from individual donors and uses grassroots, neighbor-to-neighbor tactics in order to create real change in regard to children's exposure to housing hazards. While the Peer Education Program has remained small, it is steady. In addition to this program, there is the Parents for Healthy Homes Program, in which parents who have children affected by home health hazards organize to create better solutions. By using grassroots methods, rather than hiring outsiders to do drop-in organizing, we create a community that is tied together and able to adapt to the uniqueness of each situation. I appreciate that as a community, we're learning together.

The Problem Is More Complicated

Through coalition building and grassroots tactics that connect people affected by lead, Healthy Homes and its partners are able to create real community change that results in better outcomes for families. But addressing lead in homes is not enough. Issues with lead are tied to a whole slew of other problems, including multi-generational cycles of poverty, racism, asthma and other health problems, limited access to fresh food, housing scarcity or rising housing costs, landlord disputes, and, as we saw in the example above, infestation from pests. Additionally, people who are at risk for home health hazards and lead exposure are particularly vulnerable to the current housing crisis in Grand Rapids that is exemplified by skyrocketing rent prices and the gentrification of neighborhoods in the face of rapid development.

As we learn more about how these issues are intertwined, new programs and groups have arisen to try to deal with them. For example, there is a now a Grand Rapids chapter of Homes for All that brings people and organizations together from a variety of different issue backgrounds to target specific community needs. They have two work groups. One focuses on creating a tenant union to help protect renter's rights, and the other addresses development without displacement to ensure that growth is responsible and respectful to every member of our city instead of taking advantage of poor and neglected areas as easy targets for profit.

The Fight Must Grow as Well

I've lived in Grand Rapids most of my life; I love this place dearly. I've watched as this city has changed and grown at a dramatic rate, particularly over the last fifteen years. From this are congratulatory echoes of how well we've recovered from the recession. With every "revitalized" neighborhood comes an increased risk of lead poisoned children due to unsafe renovation practices (our rate of poisonings has risen for the first time in a decade), and every new apartment and condo building erected increases the risk that our community members, who have held down the spaces ignored for so long, will be forced out.

Own the responsibility of protecting every member of our city, not just your family or the people in your immediate community. Lead is a problem across our country. As are toxic homes, homelessness, and gentrification. But most of all, our country has been poisoned by indifference.

Expanding Choices for Expanding Bellies: Growing the Midwifery Community in Grand Rapids

by Sara Badger

I had been a midwife in California for seven years when I moved to Grand Rapids in 2007. I had two small children and wasn't interested in working as a midwife here, at least not yet. I did no research into midwifery in Michigan before we moved other than to know it was legal. My husband and I had been trying for baby number three for about three years when we moved here and we quickly found ourselves pregnant two months after we arrived.

That was when I learned that the choices for maternal and prenatal care here in Grand Rapids were awful. You had the Medical Mile or three home birth midwives. That was it. For a big town, it was shocking. The midwifery culture was hidden and it was not easy to find the midwives. There was a younger midwife who was just starting out and two older midwives trained in the 1970s. Although all of them are very nice, I chose to have my baby unassisted. I had had my other two that way, but in California I was able to find a provider to do prenatal care for me and that wasn't happening here.

Fast forward to 2009. I had been to nursing groups and I had heard moms complain about their available pregnancy and labor choices. One night I was relaying the details of my day and the heartbreaking stories I had heard from women to my husband and he looked me straight in the eyes and said, "There's the sparkle in your eye! I thought it was gone! You need to help these women have choices!" We then talked over all the shifts that would have to happen in our lives for that to work!

First, I had not attended a birth in a few years and, in California, I worked as part of a team rather than alone. I asked the younger midwife I had met here in Grand Rapids if I could attend a few births with her. She said yes and put me in touch with two of her clients. With the first client, I missed the midwife's phone call and she had her assistant go instead. The next client was a lady down the street from me and, thankfully, I did get the call to go to her labor. I got to the house and the baby was born quickly before the other midwife arrived. I didn't even have time to get out my supplies! It was fast and simple.

I now felt that I was ready to jump in and I had some work to do to make this birth community ready for more choices. We needed to talk about choices and start a dialogue so more women knew they had options.

I started talking to a local theatre to see if we could host a movie and panel talk there to begin educating the public on midwifery. I worked with Jes Kramer at Wealthy Theatre and she was so helpful and knowledgeable that we ended up doing three more educational movie events. At the first movie, we raised over $1000 for a birth center in the Philippines. It started a huge community conversation! I was so excited.

During this same time frame, I was trying so hard to find someone in the local hospitals to work with us on transfer protocol and I was being shut out over and over. In the early part of 2013, the Certified Nurse Midwives (CNM) group at our local hospital announced that they would be leaving. This created a huge uproar as they were the only middle ground for women wanting a less medical hospital birth. It raised a huge question in the birth community. How could women who wanted a birth that blended a natural childbirth experience with the medical convenience of a hospital get care? The answer was to open a birth house, so I found a building to open one. I did not choose to use the term "birth center" because the local hospitals were calling their birthing floors birth centers. I wanted it to be like a home, not like a hospital. We knew it wouldn't be easy, because several midwives had tried to open one before and it had always been shot down because of zoning. But we persevered and in June 2014, we were up and going! I was the first person to have successfully opened an Out Of Hospital (OOH) birthing place in Grand Rapids.

Now that we had the Birth House up and running, I wanted to return to the problem of a lack of transfer protocols in the local hospitals. In August 2014, I met a nurse during a doula birth who would help change the conversation with the hospital. We set up transfer protocols and the change was so great! Finally, we could transfer our patients without fear of how they would treat our clients or us! They worked with us as respectfully as I could ask for at the time! Our relationship with them has grown and changed over the last couple years. We hit growing pains for sure, but the commitment to being a team has always been a priority for me and so I continue to work on communication. I am thankful to Spectrum Health for being willing to work on that relationship as well. Most nurses and the doctors have continued to be open and helpful.

2015 was harder in the midwifery community because the Michigan House of Representatives finally decided to move on the long-awaited bill that would affect the licensing of midwives in the state. It meant changes in a big way and unknown changes at that. Regulation across the country meant huge constraints to care and more work for the midwives. This was not a welcome thing for most of our midwifery community as it would eliminate midwifery services for groups of women, especially those that fell outside of the "normal" birth spectrum, including VBAC (Vaginal Birth after Cesarean), women having twins, and breech birth. I did everything I could to change the direction away from unnecessary increased licensing for the three years prior to this bill being introduced. Samantha Breaux and I put together a plan to create regulations that would actually work for the midwifery community and a volunteer certification system that had been modeled in other states. We educated people, wrote letters, and even met with the lieutenant governor, but we could not prevent the bill from passing. The group of midwives who pushed so hard for this bill has promised that they will not let it negatively impact midwifery services in Michigan, but I am not convinced.

2015 held other, more local, hardships too. There was dissent amongst the midwives in Grand Rapids. One midwife, in particular, was attacking our birth center. She made complaint after complaint, finally causing the zoning board to get involved. They told us that we had to make the bottom duplex ADA compliant in order to keep operating. The cost was too much for us or our landlord. I just couldn't continue with all the negativity in the community. I want collaboration, not competition. I was tired and didn't have any more fight left. We closed the Birth House in January 2016. The heartache was so hard and the grief was so heavy. I walked away and just did home births and settled into a new space.

And then opportunity came knocking. Cory, who owns the Old Goat and a few other restaurants in town, sat down with me to talk through some business issues and he suggested that a building across the street from the Old Goat would be perfect for a new birth center. As soon as he suggested it, my energy was back! I could do it again and now I knew what to do for zoning and coding. I immediately began working with a realtor and contractor. I found a house after looking at thirty or forty of them. I loved it and it was in my price range and a month later it was mine! Cory and I had sat down in April and the house was mine in July.

The transition happened fast! There were some bumps in the road, however. We had more problems with the zoning board (they are very lovely people, but rules in zoning are not always clear, nor do they translate into real estate) and I had to attend board meetings to fight for a zoning variance. We had to stop construction and wait for approval. The only opposition was from a fellow midwife. That was especially hard because, in the midwifery community, we believe that we are part of a sisterhood and her behavior was trying to take away choices from our community. Thankfully, the board was only looking for neighbors who took issue with us in that location so we were passed and ready to go on with construction. Once we got past these issues, my contractor and I worked our butts off to get the Birth House finished and, on October 16, 2016 (my birthday!) it was complete. We had clients lined up to give birth starting in November.

Grand Rapids had a Birth House once again and women had choices. I couldn't have been more proud. Doctors who pulled the bait and switch no longer had power over VBAC moms, forcing them to follow crazy protocols in order to achieve a vaginal birth. Women having breech babies now had choices, rather than having to get a C-section, which is still the standard across the US despite evidence that suggests it is better to try a vaginal birth. We have the ability to do Pap smears for those women not wanting to see an obstetrician (OB) or for women who have been "fired" by their obstetrician for wanting midwifery care.

As most women do not know that their doctor can "fire" them, let me take a moment to explain. Midwives work with women and explain all the risks and let the parents choose what actions or procedures they want or feel comfortable with. Most doctors (not all) here believe that co-care leaves them open to a higher risk, so instead of working with clients who might want to see both a midwife and an OB, they will "fire" you if they find out that you are thinking of a home birth. For example, in the case of a baby who is breech, midwives would try to encourage the baby to move and then talk over the true risks without judgment or fear. I have had parents choose to go in for a C-section and others stay home and still others go to the hospital and stand their ground for a vaginal breech birth. Collaboration is still a new thing to the medical groups here, but we are slowly making progress together through education on what midwifery is, how we are educated, and what our guidelines and protocols are for patient care and emergency situations.

It has been a long and sometimes hard road, but we are finally coming to a great place. I finally feel like I'm in the right place. I feel like I'm able to be a support to women in many of their birth choices: home, birth house, and hospital. I am able to continue creating new conversations around women's rights and reproductive autonomy. Motherhood is such a hard time physically and emotionally, with tons of changes and choices. We women have a ton to learn in a short amount of time, and I am honored to help women learn about themselves and grow as a family. I really love what I do!

In the ten years that I have been here, our community has grown to eleven midwives and the doula community has bloomed into the hundreds! Doulas are emotional and physical support for women in labor or during postpartum care and are an important part of birth and labor options for women. I'm so proud of the growth Grand Rapids has embraced and I hope to see it continue. One day I hope to see obstetricians and Certified Professional Midwives working together more so that women can have access to the care that they want and are comfortable with regardless of where and how they want to give birth. I hope, as a community, we can do a better job helping women rest and heal in the first weeks post-birth. I hope that postpartum care and pediatric care for women and babies who have chosen alternative birth methods become more non-judgmental and accessible. We need these things to grow healthy families and a better world.

Finding My Progressive Community

by Melissa Anderson

As a liberal transplant from the East Coast, I spent the better part of my first two decades in Grand Rapids keeping my head down, working, and raising a family, until the Progressive Women's Alliance (PWA) came along in 2004 and I found my people. Over the next seven years, I became increasingly involved in this brand-new grassroots organization, including serving as its board chairperson from 2007 to 2010. The opportunity to be part of PWA's development and growth into an influential force in the Michigan political landscape, to finally have an outlet for my political energies, and to actively engage with the community, was life-changing for me and deeply fulfilling.

My husband and I met in graduate school at the University of Michigan and moved to his hometown of Grand Rapids in 1986. I was a liberal northeasterner and developed an impression of West Michigan that may have included stereotypes, but they weren't all wrong. My sense was that the local population was much more socially conservative, church-bound, and narrow in its experience than what I was used to. We settled in Cascade Township, in part because it was similar to the semi-rural town where I grew up in Connecticut. Every Election Day served to quantify the extent to which my philosophies about the role of government and our collective responsibility to one another and to the common good were a minority viewpoint. I resigned myself to not being represented by my elected officials, and to focusing on the more immediate concerns of career and children.

In early 2004, an acquaintance told me about a new organization, a political action committee (PAC) called the Progressive Women's Alliance of West Michigan (PWA).[1] She persuaded me to buy a ticket to its first fundraiser, held on May 24, 2004, featuring Michigan's first female governor, Democrat Jennifer Granholm, who had been in office just over a year. An article in the Grand Rapids Press later quoted Governor Granholm as saying that when she was invited to speak to a group of progressive women in Grand Rapids, she thought, "Okay, thirty women or so." When she walked into the room of more than 450 people at the University Club in downtown Grand Rapids, her first words were, "Unbelievable...What's going on here? Am I in the right place?"

Governor Granholm and I had the same reaction—wow! I was impressed by the crowd, and also by the fact that I ran into a couple neighbors that I didn't know were at my end of the political spectrum. If you see yourself as a minority, you don't take the risk of speaking up, but here was a safe space with like-minded people in significant numbers. Maybe Grand Rapids was my community too, after all. News accounts said the Granholm event netted $30,000 for this new PAC, and called PWA a force to be reckoned with. I wanted to learn more about this new organization.

It turns out that, while some of us were squelching our political views, other women were gearing up to make an impact. As the PWA website says,

> "In the fall of 2003, a group of West Michigan women who were motivated to respond to the lack of progressive candidates and policies in the area formed the Progressive Women's Alliance of West Michigan (PWA). These women combined their considerable experience with political fundraising and organizing civic activities to establish West Michigan's first and only women-led, non-partisan, independent, and multi-issue political action committee (PAC) dedicated to progressive issues."

That description sounds pretty straightforward, but for founders Noreen Myers, Bette Sebastian, Joan Bowman, Kate Pew Wolters, and the rest of the initial cadre of fourteen women, creating a PAC from the ground up was a huge undertaking, even considering their formidable qualifications from years of experience with campaigns, speaker forums, community contacts, and list-building. Over those first months, their tasks included: articulating a statement of values and a policy agenda; developing criteria for candidate endorsement and financial support; defining a process to evaluate candidates applying for PWA's support; registering as a political action committee with the Michigan Department of State and Federal Elections

Commission; commencing the required financial record-keeping and reporting; writing bylaws to define how the organization would be structured and would operate; starting a listserv and website to communicate with members; and more. The work was ongoing, even as PWA launched its efforts publicly in early 2004, an impressive feat illustrating the adage, "If you want something done, give it to a busy woman."

The time was right for their project. My experience of learning about the Progressive Women's Alliance through word of mouth was being replicated hundreds of times over. Many women in Grand Rapids were frustrated with President George W. Bush and the national political scene, and were primed to find something to rally around in response. The founders of PWA offered a combination of education and advocacy that was unique for a PAC and appealed to women just finding their way into political activism.

I was one of the women flocking to the monthly events that PWA began holding in the spring of 2004, at 5:00 P.M. on the third Wednesday of each month at the Women's City Club on Fulton Street in downtown Grand Rapids. These free events provided time to network and form relationships, followed by a noteworthy speaker on a topic of current political or public policy interest. At the end of the meetings, PWA committees (e.g., Candidate, Communications, Fundraising, Membership) reported on their activities and solicited volunteers to join in the work of the organization. Many hands and talents were needed and welcome if people wanted to get involved.

In addition to attending regularly and enjoying the high-powered speakers and camaraderie, I began working with a couple of committees. I also responded to a call to help campaign for a political newcomer and PWA endorsee, Rosalynn Bliss, who was running for a seat as Second Ward City Commissioner. This was the first of what was to become many experiences going door-to-door to tell voters about a deserving candidate and her platform. (And, of course, it was the first of many successes for Rosalynn, who won in 2005, was re-elected twice, and then elected as the first woman mayor of Grand Rapids in 2015.) When a PWA book club was formed at the beginning of 2005, I began helping Meg Sorensen organize and run that activity, which brought me to the attention of the board of directors. I was invited to join the PWA board at the beginning of 2006, and elected as board chair in 2007.

I saw my role as helping the organization manage the wave of success that the founders had set in motion. The rush of enthusiasm from the community brought more people, more ideas and suggestions, more money, and more requests! It was not unusual for new ideas and requests to require new decisions by PWA's Board, so we spent much time continuing to define the organization. Would male candidates be endorsed? What geographic range would we cover? Could we partner on an event with a nonprofit organization? How should we handle interest in forming affiliates in other cities? When was it time to hire some administrative help? The questions and opportunities kept on coming.

As a PAC, PWA's primary goal was to raise money and support progressive candidates at all levels of government. Women are less likely to make political contributions, a dynamic that PWA has sought to change. In its first year, PWA raised more than $36,000, a phenomenal achievement that enabled significant campaign contributions and attracted a great deal of attention in political circles. The next year, PWA raised $50,000 through membership dues and special events, such as the August 4, 2005, fundraiser featuring US Senator Debbie Stabenow. In the presidential election year of 2008, we raised almost $80,000. PWA became known across the state as a valuable resource; political powers-that-be in Lansing were regularly referring candidates to this great new group of progressive women in Grand Rapids.

The reaction of other entities in Grand Rapids was not always as positive. It is not surprising that a political party, for example, or an individual campaign might see PWA as competition for volunteers and dollars. From my personal perspective, it seemed more likely PWA had the effect of growing the pie, since I myself had never donated to or worked with the local Democratic party. The membership of PWA, which grew from approximately sixty-five in early 2004 to 800 in the first four years, included many political newcomers in addition to longtime local political operatives.

A facet of the Progressive Women's Alliance of West Michigan that, as chairperson, I was regularly buttonholed over, was its unshakable commitment to a Values and Policy Agenda that included the statement: "We are committed to the right of privacy to make choices regarding reproduction." PWA's strong pro-choice stance meant that some progressive candidates did not meet our qualifications for endorsement. Local political leaders would argue with me that it held PWA back from being as effective as it could otherwise be, since some Democratic candidates felt the region was too conservative to elect pro-choice representatives. Nevertheless, we persisted. If some local candidates could not be supported, there were more than enough opportunities to identify qualified State House and Senate candidates elsewhere. After all, in the state legislature, a vote is a vote, so the broader aims of PWA to influence public policy could be met by backing winners in other parts of Michigan.

In its first fourteen years, PWA has helped elect and reelect many female office holders, including Michigan's first woman senator, Debbie Stabenow, Michigan's first woman governor, Jennifer Granholm, Grand Rapids's first woman mayor, Rosalynn Bliss, and District Seventy-six's first woman state representative, Winnie Brinks. It has hosted compelling educational programs and speakers, including: former UN Ambassador Richard Holbrooke; Ellen Malcolm, co-founder of EMILY's List; Lynn Sweet, Washington Bureau Chief for the Chicago Sun-Times; Kerry Eleveld, LGBTQ activist, journalist, and author; and Kary Moss, Executive Director, ACLU of Michigan. The efforts of the Progressive Women's Alliance have expanded to include two affiliate groups, on the lakeshore and in Kalamazoo.

As an active member and leader of the PAC for two two-year terms, from 2007 to 2010, I enjoyed a tremendous variety of volunteer activities. In committee work, I wrote issue briefs, authored monthly e-mails to the membership, participated in the design of a new website, and planned programs. I sold tickets to fundraisers, staffed a voter registration table at street fairs, moderated countless meetings, and appeared on a half-hour television program called Newsmakers. I donated money and knocked on doors in campaigns for at least twelve candidates, from city commissioner up to US president. I loved being on the PWA Board with all these dedicated and interesting women. It was hard—there were thorny issues and resource constraints, strong personalities and opposing viewpoints—and it was fun. I came to have a much better appreciation of the Grand Rapids community. It was a privilege, and I am grateful to have had the opportunity to be in the middle of the whirlwind that is the Progressive Women's Alliance of West Michigan.

---

1. The founders whose vision to create a unique, independent, and progressive organization has sustained PWA for over fourteen years are: Christine Albertini, Micki Benz, Joan Bowman, Sharon Handy, Phyllis Hooyman, Kathy Humphrey, Helga Kleinschmidt, Deb Mankoff, Noreen Myers, Kate Pew Wolters, Bette Sebastian, Cindy Sharp, Meg Sorensen, and Melvene Tardy.

A Journey to Activism

...where we discover why people take action

I Was a Child Feminist

by Lillian Reed

I was a child feminist.
I was the kid walking down Eastern, pigtails high on my head,
protesting. I knew the power I had. The signs I held up were there
for a reason. I was influenced by such beautiful amazing people,
and I knew it.
I was a child and I was educated.
I was the kid in the second grade class that could tell you each individual part of the vulva and its purpose. As children we are taught
to be ashamed of the female body, but I embraced it. I was taught to
question what I didn't believe in, and fight for what I did.
I was a child, and I was empowered.
I walked downtown in my blue skirt and sneakers screaming at
the top of my lungs for the rights of my fellow females to do as
they wish with their bodies, at ten years old.
I am a teen activist, and I still fight.

*I wrote this poem about my childhood. I was pretty young when I remember starting as
a volunteer with Planned Parenthood. I had such great memories protesting and helping
women who need it. I had fun.*

*I was inspired by the people I grew up with. I was inspired by my mom. I was inspired by
women. I wanted to channel that happiness when I was writing the poem. I wanted others
to feel the same power that just being with those women gave me. I wanted others to understand that age doesn't matter anymore, that you can make a difference just by being there
for others. Especially in this time.*

A City of Women with Wings
by *Elizabeth D. Barnum*

I moved to Grand Rapids from New England in 2013. People often ask why I moved here. I begin by saying, "for a job at Fountain Street Church," and then add, "I was feeling too New England for California and too California for New England, so I thought I'd give the Midwest a try." Before the move, I'd done my research on Grand Rapids. I was starting to catch on that it was a small city with big impact, an increasingly must-visit place, and that there was a creative tide sweeping its streets.

Soon after I arrived, I started crossing paths with activists who were putting their hearts and souls into connecting people with one another to do the hard and rewarding work of building community. In addition to the many members of the congregation I serve, I had the chance to get to know people like Katherine Baker, Katie Gordon, Lyza Ingraham, Jenny Kinne, and Dani Vilella, to name just a few Grand Rapidians who are making a difference. I'd witnessed the work of the Fountain Street Church Choice Fund and community partners like the Grand Rapids chapter of the National Organization of Women and Planned Parenthood Advocates of Michigan. Conversations over coffee or lunch with other female ministers in town would be sources of refuge and organizing. My life of faith would be nourished by programs at the Dominican Center at Marywood. I'd be moved by the voices of women invited to be part of the ecumenical Christian faith symposium, "Opening the Stained Glass Window," offered by the Red Cord Community.

The religious, theological, political, and spiritual landscape of Grand Rapids is diverse and that diversity is only expanding. Interfaith dialogue and intra-faith relations continue to increase, as do opportunities for seekers, skeptics, and those who identify as spiritual-but-not-religious, to be part of a wider community that allows for both affinity and difference. Regardless of some of those affinities and differences, I meet people every day working to make Grand Rapids a place that all people can call home with pride. These many groups and individuals inspire me to keep doing the work I do as a minister and a feminist. I'm often described as unique in my identity as a liberal religious feminist but I'm not the only one. There are more than a few of us. The voices of female religious leadership have a long history in this city and another movement is just beginning.

On January 21, 2017, there was a swell of activism across the nation and planet as people of all genders marched in support of the Women's March on Washington. Fountain Streeter Kristen Loch and my colleagues organized five buses of West Michiganders to travel to DC. I stayed behind in Grand Rapids, where the sanctuary of Fountain Street Church welcomed speakers, musicians, and artists, in addition to providing a live stream of the Women's March. The following words are the remarks I shared from the pulpit on that historic day:

Good afternoon. I am Rev. Elizabeth Barnum, one of the ministers here at Fountain Street Church. On behalf of my colleagues and the congregation, I welcome you to this sanctuary. If this is your first time in this place and if you are looking for a community that will support you in the work ahead of us as a city, state, nation, and world, I invite you to come back again. Learn more about how you can become engaged in the work of this church, in activism and healing, in learning and sharing.

Today is my ten-year ordination anniversary. If there is one comment that I've had said to me most often in the past decade, it is, "you don't look like a minister." It doesn't always make sense to people that minister, Christian, woman, and feminist could all be part of one's identity—add to that progressive or liberal, and people don't quite know what to make of a person.

I was ordained in one of the denominations that has a rich history of shattering the stained glass ceiling and ordaining women early on in the movement. However, in a magazine published for women across the denomination that arrived in my mailbox this week, there was a two-page spread highlighting the voices of women sharing some of the sexism, blatant and subtle, still prevalent not only in churches, but in our world. The title of the spread? "Still Dealing with It."

We are still dealing with it. And we will still be dealing with it, unfortunately, at increased levels in our nation in the years ahead. The divisions within our communities and country are real: sexism, racism, ageism, ableism, classism. Categories that seek to identify us become fears that divide us. The fears looming are real and many, including ongoing threats to reproductive justice and to a woman's full capacity for moral agency.

So where do we get our strength for the long haul? I turn to our foremothers. One of the more influential essays I read as a seminary student was written by theologian and feminist Beverly Harrison entitled, "The Power of Anger in the Work of Love." I'm going to take the liberty to read an excerpt from it now.

"Anger is not the opposite of love. It is better understood as a feeling-signal that all is not well in our relation to other persons or groups or to the world around us...To grasp this point—that anger signals something amiss in relationship—is a critical first step in understanding the power of anger in the work of love." [1]

Today, we are reminded of what nourishes us for the long haul: gathering in community, learning about the issues that matter, finding our voices, recognizing anger as fuel for a loving justice.

We are reminded that the long road of protest, healing, and justice requires not only hard work, but also requires the beauty of connection with others, the words of poetry, the creation and experience of art, and the songs that inspire us to feel the full range of human emotion and to ultimately abide in hope.

At the girls' summer camp where I spent many summers as a child, there was a chant that we sang one Sunday at an outdoor chapel service. Years later, I haven't forgotten the words. As I think of the thousands gathering in Washington, DC, today for the Women's March on Washington and all over this country, I can still hear the words of that chant:

"There's a river of birds in migration, a nation of women with wings." [2]

May it be so. It is so. Rise up, friends.

Grand Rapids is a city of women with wings.

1. Harrison, Beverly. *"The Power of Anger in the Work of Love: Christian Ethics for Women and Other Strangers"* in Weaving the Visions: New Patterns in Feminist Spirituality, edited by Judith Plaskow and Carol Christ, (San Francisco: Harper, 1989).

2. Libana Lyrics, Migration Song (Spinning Records, 1986).

Seeing Grand Rapids
by Kelley Climie

Something happens.

Something happens in Grand Rapids.

Something happens in Grand Rapids and we want to help.

We reach out to a friend, or a friend of a friend, or someone better connected than we are.

We reach out and we say, "I want to help. How can I do that?"

We get involved. We offer what we can.

The above scenario is common in Grand Rapids.

I found myself going through these motions, but one occasion gave me pause. Well, no, not a just a pause. One occasion grabbed a hold of me, and has stirred something within me.

Something happened in Grand Rapids.

I reached out to a friend. The friend was better connected. The better-connected friend reached out to a co-worker involved in the thing that happened in Grand Rapids.

The email connecting us went like this:

> A meet B.
>
> B is an activist in the Grand Rapids area.
>
> B can help with X.
>
> A, I am hoping you can connect with B.
>
> Regards,
> The Better-Connected Friend

I read this email and felt a kind of terror brew within me as I fixated on one line of the email:

"B is an activist in the Grand Rapids area."

Activist? Me? Oh, no.

The better-connected friend had it all wrong. The better-connected friend had me all wrong. I'm not an activist. Am I? I just wanted to help. Oh, no. The involved co-worker is going to think I am more qualified to assist than I am.

I've fooled them. I'm a fraud. I want to hide. Why did I even say anything?

The response back from the better-connected friend yielded none of the attack or suspicion I had been anticipating. We exchanged details on how I could help, and I helped, and I spread the word to others.

This situation is still with me, and I suspect this situation is familiar to many of us in Grand Rapids.

Why was I so fearful of being called an activist?

Why did I feel like a fraud who would be found out?

I am not sure that I fully understand this phenomenon. Imposter Syndrome? Lack of confidence?

But in Grand Rapids, I suspect these insecurities loom heavily over some of our most compassionate people.

I suspect that the discomfort with being referred to as an "activist" in Grand Rapids is because we feel that we are never doing enough, or that what we are doing is not as impactful as it needs to be.

Kent County, and specifically the Grand Rapids area, is home to numerous nonprofit organizations and grassroots community efforts. Yet, despite our resources, residents experience stark inequity.

Activists in Grand Rapids know this.

We know that we have more resources in Kent County and in the Grand Rapids area than many other counties and cities in Michigan, and yet it's not enough. We feel our resources are not enough, and that we are not enough.

While issues within the city persist, it's hard to pat yourself or someone else on the back. There is so much to be done. There is so much we are not doing. There are too many voices that have been left out of the conversation. There is so much we have not accounted for.

Personal anecdote:

I am a second generation Cuban American. My mother Maria, her parents Julio and Dulce, and her siblings Dulce, Ana, and Rita arrived in the United States in 1967 (twin boys Frank and Walter were born shortly after). I am still trying to understand what being a second generation Cuban American means for me, but what I have come to understand is that my personal desire to "help" and my anxiety about not "doing enough" and what "resilience" I do have I credit to my mother Maria, my Cuban relatives, and those friends, family members, professors, neighbors, residents, and fellow activists who have shared their stories of feelings of helplessness and resilience.

I mention this because, from where I am standing in Grand Rapids, it is our stories and our support of one another that is ultimately the strongest hand we have to play.

My hope for Grand Rapids's activists is that we continue to personally and collectively examine where the source of our desires lie, where our anxiety, insecurity, and apprehension stems from, and by what means we can and do sustain our resiliency.

Why? Because understanding ourselves and listening to one another is essential if we are going to continue to put in the work necessary to strengthen our community. We know this, but when time and energy are limited, it is difficult to ward off how overwhelming the needs are, and how inadequate we feel to provide or aid in the solution.

We need to remind ourselves and one another, especially in those overwhelming and frustrating moments, why our city is worth fighting for.

What I love about Grand Rapids is that when I am feeling overwhelmed, frustrated, angry, when I feel that my cup is empty, someone will be singing or playing the guitar in Rosa Parks Circle or on someone's porch or in someone's living room. Someone will be throwing a house show, and collecting donations in a jar to give to the bands. Someone will be performing at a venue and their friends will be running the merch table, designing t-shirts or album cover art and buttons. Someone will be getting coffee and planning a neighborhood summer celebration, or a youth camp, or an art market. Someone will be hosting a potluck for friends they've had little time to see. Someone will be hosting an engagement party at a home or art studio for their friends who can't afford to rent a venue. Someone will be hosting a book club. Someone will be trying to organize volunteers and meals to help a friend with an illness or someone who has experienced the loss of a loved one. Someone is organizing a tip-sharing group among those in the bar and service industry (those whose wages are inconsistent and often without benefits themselves) to raise funds for local nonprofits. Someone will be trying to organize rides or supplies after a tragic event. Someone will be mobilizing, in whatever way they can.

Who are our activists in Grand Rapids?

Our activists are servers, bartenders, home health aides, students, herbalists, gardeners, home brewers, translators, readers, musicians, community radio volunteer hosts, house show curators, artists, prep-cooks, line-cooks, dishwashers, neighborhood association staff, social workers, community organizers, retail cashiers, hair stylists, jewelry makers, print makers, filmmakers, tattoo artists, baristas, midwives, mural artists, administrative assistants, parents, barbacks, yoga instructors, car insurance agents, IT specialists, graphic designers, teachers, library and museum staff, and many more.

Our activists are many of these occupations and callings and talents all at once. Our activists are carving out time and energy that they don't have to find some way to be involved.

We are attempting to heal ourselves and one another.

We are sometimes so caught up in the anger and the fatigue of the pulsing inequity that we feel insufficient to push against it in our city.

Our neighborhoods are changing, often without resident input or support. Housing costs are dramatically increasing while wages remain stagnant. Transportation is limited in routes and its schedules are often too unreliable for employers to deem adequate for hopeful job seekers. Neighbors vary in access to grocery stores, farmers markets, and restaurants with affordable and healthy meal options. The impacts of becoming "Beer City, USA" is a conversation we need to broaden; what does it mean to become a destination city for alcohol at a time when residents, neighborhoods, and health and mental health organizations are struggling to adequately support those impacted by substance use? Grand Rapids is home to ArtPrize, offering huge cash payouts to artists who may or may not be from our state or city, and yet our children have scant art supplies in their public schools or after-school programs. And on and on...

This small list barely scratches the surface.

We criticize ourselves and one another, demanding that we do better and be better, while at the same time we are investigating self-care, self-compassion, safe-space, and compassion for others.

We are not perfect. We are not experts.

And yet...

Something happens.

Something happens in Grand Rapids and we want to help.

Something happens in Grand Rapids and we get connected and we give what little time and emotional energy we have and we try.

Activists in Grand Rapids are unlikely to call themselves activists.

While I am no authority, you, activists of Grand Rapids, are what keep me going.

You are why I stay in this city.

You are not frauds. You are enough.

I see you, activists of Grand Rapids, and I thank you.

From Disability Advocacy to Food Justice

by Jorja Jankowski

I lived in Grand Rapids from 2006 to 2016. Ten years living, working, and organizing in the city.

I have always been an activist in some fashion—usually on disability issues, empowering people of all abilities to accomplish their hopes and dreams. I use a wheelchair myself, and I have encountered discrimination most of my life, which has driven my passion for promoting and advancing social equality for others and myself. This essay focuses on my journey from disability advocate to social work student to community organizer.

I have experienced and witnessed a lot of discrimination—in Grand Rapids and elsewhere. It has not deterred me from living a life of inclusion, and wanting to help others despite my condition.

I say "despite" because, for my whole adult life, I have been told that I am an inspiration, and asked daily, "How do you get up every morning and make it to work on time?" My response: "Isn't that what you are supposed to do? Get out of bed, make it to work on time, and make a difference in the world?"

I have never seen myself as someone who physically struggles in everyday life. I see myself as someone who is open-minded, empathetic, and with a lot to offer the world. I have a unique perspective on life; I am not "different," I just use a wheelchair.

***

When I moved to Grand Rapids in 2006, I figured that I would continue making a difference by advocating for self-determination within the disability community. I had worked for nonprofits for years before coming to Grand Rapids. The nonprofits I had worked with in the past tended to be progressive and open-minded institutions. Therefore, I thought I would be welcomed with open arms in Grand Rapids's nonprofit community as well.

I had years of experience. I should have been welcomed.

I was in for a culture shock. I was flabbergasted by the negative response I received from employers and the public of Grand Rapids. I have lived all over the country, making a positive impact on people, yet felt like an outsider in the Grand Rapids community since I did not grow up here. Also, there was not an active disability community to be found. I went into problem-solving mode; I enrolled in the master of Social Work (MSW) program at Grand Valley State University so I would be taken seriously in the future, maybe?

"Maybe," I thought, "I would bring a positive energy and awareness to the disability community."

During graduate school, I discovered community social work. It was the perfect fit, building on my program leadership experience. I could develop a program and still have one-on-one time with clients.

It was also in graduate school that I learned about neighborhood and community development. Community development is where members of a community, be it a neighborhood or an identity-group, come together to take collective action and generate solutions to common issues. The process tends to evolve from grassroots action directed at local problems, such as demanding a safer neighborhood or organizing resources for children.

After graduate school, I served in AmeriCorps. AmeriCorps is a civil society program supported by the US federal government that engages adults in public service work with a goal of fostering civic engagement and meeting critical needs in the community. I could put my program leadership and community development skills into practice. I was mainly on the west side of Grand Rapids, helping neighbors. In line with the principles of AmeriCorps, I engaged and educated neighbors on preventative health care, as well as helped to enroll families in state Medicaid programs.

There were six of us serving in the west side center office. While engaging with the families, we discovered what the community really wanted and needed. Each day we would come together, trying to make sense of the issues and challenges presented to us by community residents, trying to figure out how to help.

I remember on a few occasions that a mother or a family member would come into the office to apply for health insurance for their child. In the midst of our conversations, the topic of food, or lack thereof for the household, would come up. Mom would ask if I knew where to get food to last a week or so because the MI Bridges card had a zero balance and the designated food pantry had strict guidelines. Also, a variety of nutritious food was not available. Those were the main issues I heard.

I began looking at their addresses, as well as their transportation resources. Where were families getting their food? At what cost? How much hassle was it to get food from a food pantry? Was the MI Bridge card allowance sufficient for a whole family for thirty days, especially within the inner core of Grand Rapids? The answers to these questions were alarming and discouraging.

Our group began to identify that the community wanted and needed better access to nutritious food to promote healthier lifestyles. We heard time and time again from families that they did not like buying food at a liquor store, nor spending three hours on a bus to Meijer. Neighbors stated they wanted a better option to obtain food, yet did not know or have the means to acquire it. The food pantries were (and are) extremely limited; therefore, the neighbors were at a loss.

The residents of this west side neighborhood were living in a food desert; they were asking us for ways to improve food access and security.

After serving in AmeriCorps, my colleagues and I established a nonprofit to address the issues of food scarcity and nutrition. We sought to help the residents build the healthy community they desired. We knew hunger was a nationwide and worldwide issue; we had lived across the globe and saw the effects first hand. But here it was—hunger, poor health, and food insecurity—right here in Grand Rapids.

There had to be something we could do in the community where we lived.

Our philosophy was client-centered. The Grand Rapids community was not meeting people's basic human needs by providing a standardized box of food once a month from a designated food pantry. Therefore, we sought to create a system that provided people with access to food; what they wanted, when they wanted it, no questions asked.

We developed a collaboration with Feeding America.

This collaboration gave neighborhoods easier access to food via food trucks. It also created awareness for the broader community that a $10 donation to Feeding America is more beneficial than donating dry food cans to the local food pantry.

We partnered with local nonprofits, mainly in west side neighborhoods, to write grants to fund community gardens. We developed educational information on nutrition basics for neighbors. We helped neighbors build community gardens around the city's inner core. Our goal was to help neighbors build and maintain gardens that would be sustainable as well as bountiful to share with all the neighbors.

We had helped a west side neighbor build a container garden in an open lot next to her house. We had helped with the process of city approval, received donations from Rylee's Ace Hardware and local greenhouses. Our group each picked a day of the week to help with the newly developed garden. I had organized volunteers to help maintain and harvest the garden. Each week when I went to help, neighbors would be hesitant as they walked by. I took notice and said, "Hey, help yourself." I would offer a recipe for a vegetable if needed. Throughout the summer, more neighbors stopped on by, eager to help water and pull weeds. Meanwhile, I was looking around, thinking, "Yes! Neighbors coming together, no questions asked, harvesting food for their family." Plus, having fun with each other was a bonus—kids playing in the sprinklers, parents sharing recipes and food combinations.

***

Over time, I began getting more civically and politically involved within the city. I served on the board of the Midtown Neighbor-hood Association for six years, helping with public safety and neighborhood improvement efforts. I helped with the final touches of the Fulton Street Farmers Market. I helped with the revitalization of the Fulton Street Cemetery. I implement-ed fundraising efforts to aid in additional neighborhood proj-ects to increase awareness of activities and improvements of Midtown. I had a major voice in the Michigan Street Corridor Project; making sure it was neighborhood friendly, as well as wheelchair friendly for the whole community.

After ten years, I left Grand Rapids; my partner had a great career opportunity in Northern California. I would like to think I had an impact the Grand Rapids for the better; not as I expect-ed, but the universe directs you in different ways. I am happy to be a contributor to the Grand Rapids Grassroots Community.

Mi Vida, Mi Historia, Mi Narrativa

by *Reyna García*

Fase I: Mi infancia

Nací en la ciudad de México en los años setentas una época donde podíamos jugar en las calles sin ningún problema. Mi infancia fue una época hermosa donde disfruté al máximo siempre sonriendo con mis vecinos con los que eran como mi familia.

Mi padre emigró del sur de Mexico, provincia de alpoyeca en el estado de Guerrero. Salió de su lugar de origen para tener una mejor vida, un hombre humilde que siempre nos dio lo mejor que pudo, nos construyó una casa, recuerdo que siempre se levantaba temprano de madrugada y regresaba por la tarde y aun así regresaba para seguir trabajando en los deberes que fueran necesarios.

Mi madre una mujer de fe que siempre abogaba por los más necesitados. Recuerdo cuando los artesanos de las provincias pasaban y tocaban la puerta para vender su trabajo, algunas veces estaban agotados de caminar y en otras con hambre y deshidratados.

No puedo olvidar que un día mi madre pasó a la casa a una mujer indígena con su bebe porque necesitaba leche para su hijo y ella estaba acalorada, mi madre le ofreció de comer y le dio la leche necesaria a esa mujer desde ese momento sentí un dolor muy profundo por esa situación y una frustración porque no quería imaginarme como era la vida de esas personas. Mi pregunta era como puedo ayudarlos. Mi madre creía en un cambio social para mi país, me llevaba a las protestas y conocer los candidatos de la izquierda. Sabía que ella era una guerrera.

Aún tengo presente cuando asistí por primera vez a la escuela me encanto mi primer maestro de primer grado le llamábamos el maestro Panchito el me llamaba "La Campeona."

Pero un día visitando a mi tía nos quedamos a dormir a su casa y al siguiente día desperté con la novedad que no podía caminar, mis piernas estaban paralizadas me sentí desesperada por que nadie me explicó porque me estaba pasando eso. Mi madre y mi padre me dijeron que quizás saliendo al sol podría volver a caminar y en efecto después de veinticuatro horas volví a caminar lentamente desde ese momento comenzó una nueva ruta en mi vida.

La poliomielitis un virus que fue el factor que todo fuera diferente, si había sobrevivido a esta enfermedad a la cual no comprendía y mi pregunta era por qué yo?

Comencé a caminar sintiendo mi pierna izquierda difícil me caía constantemente y cuando me di cuenta ya mi pierna era diferente se deformo y comencé a usar un zapato ortopédico.

En la escuela empezaron hacerme burla y cuando caminaba por la calle me gritaban nombres se reían de mi entonces solo abrazaba a mi madre para sanar un poco el dolor de algo que no entendía.

Entonces me di cuenta que era muy creativa, siempre hacía los trabajos manuales diferentes únicos. Consideró el arte me rescato de ese dolor y de esa discriminación. Por otro lado no dejaba de jugar y disfrutar de esas tardes de risa y aventuras por soñar que algún día todo sería diferente.

Fase II: Mi adolescencia

Cuando mi cuerpo comenzó a cambiar fue difícil dejar a esa niña juguetona y ver que comenzaba una nueva etapa. Como viviría con una discapacidad en un ambiente donde no había respeto ni leyes que nos protegieran? Solo salir a la calle era un tormento y todos los días una lucha. Siempre fui una estudiante brillante eso me daba tranquilidad.

Mirarme en el espejo cada vez era ver una realidad cruel. En el noveno grado fue un tiempo de muchos retos y muchas desilusiones de como el sistema del escuela me recriminaba. No había una educación respecto al tema de la discapacidad.

Decidí abandonar la escuela por mis miedos, mi frustración de sentirme inferior a los demás no lo pude superar. Mi hermano mayor me animó a continuar estudiando en la casa hasta terminar la secundaria. Siempre agradeceré a mi hermano la oportunidad de llevarme a su escuela bachilleres para poder ir a las clases de arte con el maestro Carlos. Esta clase fue mi refugio y entendí que el arte era mi pasión.

Cuando comencé la preparatoria era otra etapa que decidí afirmarme pero sin ningún éxito mis inseguridades comenzaron, como la competencia en la moda en quien tenía novio, en quien es la más popular no la pude tolerar y entonces nuevamente no pude avanzar.

Entonces decidí que debía irme lejos, tuve la oportunidad de venir a este país gracias a un tio que me invitó a venir. Entonces pensé finalmente volveré a comenzar, sentí la libertad de ser yo de no ser juzgada, sentí un ambiente diferente cuando emigre a USA.

Fue difícil llegar a un nuevo país, un nuevo idioma otra cultura. La adaptación llegó cuando finalmente llegué a Nueva York. Conocí un grupo de jóvenes de la iglesia, realizamos muchas actividades, comencé a estudiar más el idioma y finalmente me sentí más integrada.

Fase III: Mi edad adulta

Alrededor de mis treinta años entré en una crisis de mirar el tiempo y que es lo había realizado, al mismo tiempo sabía que tenía un sueño y sabia cual era mi pasión. A esta edad finalmente descubrí que para seguir avanzando era necesario aceptarme completamente que no era el pasado, ni la gente que todo el problema era yo. Si, fue tormentoso pensar que pude haber disfrutado una adolescencia feliz sabiendo de mis fortalezas de mi capacidad de luchar por mis sueños sin importar que pensara la gente.

Ese día fue crucial llorar y reconocer que a veces todo el poder de cambiar nuestra narrativa está en nuestras manos solo es suficiente creer en nosotros mismos. Comencé una nueva etapa de liberación. Entonces comencé a tener control de mi vida, mi alma y mi espíritu.

Como madre soltera de tres hijos sabía que tenía que ser un ejemplo para ellos. Pude ver que me corresponde darles esa seguridad y hacerles saber cada día de los maravillosos seres humanos que eran. Ser madre soltera ha sido una experiencia por la que he tenido que superar muchas barreras como mujer.

He vivido experiencias de aprendizaje donde es posible avanzar cuando existen deseos de salir adelante tres veces estuve sin hogar pesé a estas situaciones visualicé mi vida para alcanzar esas metas pesé a las dificultades. En Grand Rapids he tenido la oportunidad de conocer gente maravillosa y de recibir el apoyo de organizaciones que han estado acompañándome en este camino.

Fase IV: La lucha social

El 26 de septiembre del 2014 se dió un suceso en México, la desaparición de los cuarenta y tres estudiantes de la escuela rural localizada en Ayotzinaoa, en manos del ejército y la policía de Iguala, Guerrero. Escuchar las noticias de que los familiares estaban pidiendo ayuda para encontrarlos me hizo pensar que más podía hacer aparte de llorar y sentir frustración por ellos o como evitar estas situaciones de impunidad. Mi pregunta fue qué pasaría si eso me llegaría pasar a mi, si mi hijo fuera desaparecido? Una pregunta que tocó lo más profundo de mi conciencia.

Algo comenzó a cambiar en mi era mi manera de ver la vida en cuanto a la segregación, la opresión y la corrupción de un sistema. Comencé hablar de este caso en los espacios donde me invitaban a presentar mi arte, entonces comencé a usar el término social como artista activista. El caso de los cuarenta y tres estudiantes de Ayotzinapa me dio un panorama más abierto para entender que era el capitalismo y el imperialismo y me ayudó a ver su relación con problemas sociales de actualidad tales como el crimen organizado transnacional, lavado de dinero, migración forzada y el Plan Mérida, un acuerdo de seguridad entre los gobiernos de los Estados Unidos y México bajo el pretexto de combatir el tráfico de drogas. Pero junto con ello me llenó de dolor saber que había mucho trabajo que hacer.

Comencé a organizar a la comunidad fui la co-fundadora de Justice for Ayotzinapa Grand Rapids MI. Creando un grupo de apoyo para recibir a los padres de los jóvenes desaparecidos que visitaron en la Caravana 43 a nuestra comunidad. Poder abrazar a María de Jesús Tlatempa madre de uno de los jóvenes desaparecidos y a

Cruz Bautista tío de uno de los estudiantes. Me llevó a adquirir un compromiso con la lucha social de México.

Entonces commencé a conectar con nacionalmente con más connacionales con los cuales he colaborado apoyando a las causas y conversando con las personas afectadas por la corrupción en México. Logramos apoyar para la liberación de una presa política ya que en México tenemos muchos indígenas líderes de su comunidad en las cárceles, tenemos más de veintenueve mil desaparecidos.

Actualmente estoy organizando un proyecto grassroots cultural movement, se llama "Niños del sol." Elaboré este proyecto inspirándome en mis hijos, ya que ellos siendo hijos de latinos es una nueva generación que lucha por su identidad donde como padres estamos constantemente luchando para conservar el lenguaje y su cultura.

Realmente este activismo de grassroots es financiado por las personas de la comunidad y ha sido difícil encontrar apoyo económico solo por ser liderado por una persona que no pertenece a una organización. Me he conectado con otras personas a través de las redes sociales y cuando realizó mi trabajo como Artista-activista. En mis exhibiciones es donde puedo conocer e interactuar con personas interesadas en la lucha social y tengo la oportunidad de crear redes para dar seguimiento a las conversaciones comunitarias.

En Grand Rapids aún se requiere dar más trabajo para empoderar a la comunidad. Todavía se necesita comprender cómo la comunidad latina puede comunicar el mensaje social y cómo podemos involucrar a más personas siempre y cuando tomando conciencia que es necesario hacer estrategias inteligentes, donde aún podemos ser parte de la conversación más amplia para así ser escuchados.

El ataque racial y discriminatorio constante a nuestra comunidad ha logrado que haya un ambiente de miedo e inseguridad. Creo fielmente que debemos organizarnos inteligentemente desde la comunidad para la comunidad usando nuestros recursos y talentos para fortalecer a nuestras nuevas generaciones. Ya que ellos son nuestras semillas hay que cultivarles. Como artista activista social tengo un compromiso de seguir llevando ese mensaje de esperanza. Amo a mi comunidad y agradezco a las personas, organizaciones que han confiado en mi trabajo.

La comunidad latina en Grand Rápids estamos creando un ambiente de unidad para darle a Grand Rápids un toque diverso e inclusivo. No somos extraños, los inmigrantes también podemos hacer America great!

#IloveMyCommunity.

My Life, My History, My Story: English Translation

by Reyna García

Phase I: My Childhood

I was born in Mexico City in the seventiess at a time where we could play in the streets without any problem. My childhood was a beautiful time where we always smiled at my neighbors who were like my family.

My father migrated from the southern part of Mexico, the province of Alpoyeca in the state of Guerrero. He left his home in search of a better life, a humble man who always gave us the best things he could. He built us a house where I remember him leaving early in the morning and returning in the afternoon and still taking care of chores around the house.

My mother was a woman of deep faith who always advocated for those most in need. I remember when the artisans from the province came by and knocked on our door to sell their work, sometimes they were exhausted from walking and other times they were hungry and thirsty.

I cannot forget that one day when my mother welcomed into our house an indigenous woman with her baby who needed milk for her son. She was overwhelmed by the heat and thirst, so my mother offered her food and gave her milk for the baby. From that moment on, I felt touched by that situation and also frustrated because I couldn't imagine the conditions these people lived in. I wondered how I could help them. My mother believed Mexico needed social change. She took me to public protests and to meet the political candidates from the left. I knew she was a warrior.

I still felt this when I attended school for the first time. I loved my first grade teacher. I called him "Panchito" and he called me "the champion."

But one day, visiting my aunt, we spent the night at her house and the next day when I woke up I was surprised to find out I could not walk. My legs were paralyzed so I felt desperate because nobody could explain to me what was going on. My mother and my father told me that perhaps I could walk again when the sun came out and indeed, after twenty-four hours I was able to walk slowly, and from that moment on I began a new journey in my life.

The polio virus was the factor that changed everything. I had to survive this disease which I did not understand and I kept asking "Why me?"

I slowly started walking, feeling my left leg get hardened and I fell down constantly. When I realized my leg was different and it got deformed, I started to wear an orthopedic shoe.

Kids began to mock me in school and when I was walking down the street people would call me names. They would laugh at me and only the hugs of my mother could heal the pain of something I still didn't quite understand.

Then I realized I was very creative. At school I always made craftwork that was very different and unique. I think the art rescued me from the pain of discrimination.

At the same time, I wouldn't stop playing and enjoying my evenings of laughter and adventure by dreaming that someday everything would be different.

Phase II: My Adolescence

As my body started to change, it was difficult to leave that playful girl behind and start experiencing a new stage. How was I to live with a disability in an environment where there was no respect and no laws that protect us? Just going out into the streets was a torment and an everyday struggle. What gave me peace of mind was that I always was a brilliant student.

To see myself in the mirror was a daily cruel reality. By the ninth grade, I confronted many challenges and many disappointments as I realized how the school system discriminated against people with disabilities. Students were not educated to appreciate or respect physical limitations.

I decided to leave school because the fear, frustration, and feeling inferiority to others were emotions I could not overcome.

My older brother encouraged me to continue studying at home and finish high school afterwards. I'll always be thankful to my brother for taking me to his preparatory school where I had the opportunity to attend art classes with Maestro Carlos. This class was my refuge and it was where I understood that art was my passion.

When I started high school, it was another stage where I decided to assert myself, but with not much success. I had to deal with the regular adolescent insecurities, such as competing for popularity and boyfriend issues. I could not tolerate the pressure and was unable to advance.

I decided then that I had to get away and I had the opportunity to come to the United States thanks to an invitation from my uncle. The new environment gave me the incentive for a new start. I felt the freedom of not being judged and I embraced the different culture one experiences immigrating to the US.

It's never an easy decision to come to a new country, learn a new language, and adopt another culture, but when I finally arrived in New York, I met a group of young people at church, where I participated in many activities, and I began to study the English language and finally began to feel appreciated and accepted.

Phase III: My Adulthood

Around the time I turned thirty years old, I needed to look at the time and evaluate what I had accomplished. At the same time, I knew I had a dream to pursue and knew what my passion was. At this age, I finally discovered that in order to move forward, it was necessary to fully accept myself, let go of the past, and realize that people were not my problem, but rather it was me who was holding myself back. It was sad to think that I could have enjoyed a happy adolescence knowing my strengths and my ability to fight for my dreams no matter what people thought.

That day was a crucial day of realization. It was important to mourn and also to recognize that sometimes all the power to change our narrative is in our hands. It's only a matter of believing in oneself. This started a new stage of liberation and I started to take control of my life, my soul, and my spirit.

As a single mother, I knew I had to be a role model for my three children.

I assumed the responsibility to reassure them every day what beautiful human beings they were. Being a single mother is an experience by which I have had to overcome many challenges as a woman.

I have lived experiences where I learned it is possible to advance as long as one has the desire to succeed. I have been homeless three times but despite these situations, I have been able to envision a life where I could achieve my goals. I have had the opportunity of meeting wonderful people in Grand Rapids and have earned the support of organizations that have accompanied me along my journey.

Phase IV: Social Struggle

On September 26, 2014, Mexico was shattered by the news of the disappearance of forty-three students from a rural teaching academy located in Ayotzinapa by members of the army and the police of Iguala, Guerrero. As I learned that the relatives were asking for help to find them, it made me wonder what I could do, aside from joining them in their mourning and feelings of frustration, in their attempts to find justice not provided by the government.

It made me question what it would feel like if the same happened to me, if one of my children went missing. This was a question that touched the depths of my conscience.

Then something began to change inside of me—it was my way of seeing life in terms of systemic segregation, oppression, and corruption. I started to talk about these issues any time I was invited to present my art, so I started to adopt the social identity of an activist-artist. The forty-three students from the Ayotzinapa case gave me a clearer view of the meaning of capitalism and imperialism and helped me understand their correlation with current social issues such as transnational organized crime, money laundering, forced migration, and the Plan Merida, a security co-operation agreement between the United States and the government of Mexico under the guise of combating drug trafficking. Along with my activism, there is an overwhelming feeling that there is much work to be done.

I began a community information and organizing campaign and became the co-founder of Justice for Ayotzinapa Grand Rapids Michigan, creating a support group for the parents of the missing students who visited our city with the Caravana 43 project in 2015. Through this, I was able to meet Maria de Jesus Tlatempa Bello, whom I embraced as one mother to another, and also Cruz Bautista, an uncle of one of the students. This opportunity helped me adopt a commitment for the social struggles of Mexico.

It was then that I started to meet and connect with more people at a national level with whom I have collaborated to promote and support the causes our people are affected by due to corruption in Mexico. We advocate for and support the release of political prisoners in Mexico. We have many indigenous and community leaders in prisons and there are more than 29,000 missing people.

As part of a local cultural movement, I am currently organizing a grassroots project I call "Children of the Sun." I developed this project, inspired by my children who are Latino, and I see it as part of a new generation fighting for their identity where we as parents constantly struggle to preserve our language and culture.

Actually, this grassroots activism is funded by people in the community and it has been difficult to find financial support being led by only one person who does not belong to an organization. I have connected with other people through social networks and through my work as an activist-artist. In my exhibits, I can meet and interact with people interested in the social struggle and it gives me the opportunity to create a network to follow-up on the community conversations

Grand Rapids still requires more work to empower the community. We still need to understand how the Latino community can communicate the social message and how it can involve more people, provided we understand it is necessary to create intelligent strategies, where we can still be part of the larger conversation in order to be heard.

The constant racist and discriminatory attacks on our community have created an atmosphere of fear and insecurity. I deeply believe we must organize strategically from within our communities by using our own resources and talents to strengthen a new generation. Since they are our seeds, we must cultivate them. As a social activist-artist, I am committed to continue carrying a message of hope. I love my community and every day I thank the people and organizations that have put their trust in my work.

The Latino community in Grand Rapids is creating an atmosphere of unity to make our city a diverse and inclusive place. Our message is that we are not strangers; as immigrants we can also make America great.

#IloveMyCommunity.

Good Enough

by Zyra Castillo

Grand Rapids is my city. It didn't always feel that way though. Many times, my fight or flight response has urged me to escape. I wanted to leave since early college, when I didn't feel like I fit into the space, place, or culture. I left the Upper Peninsula to attend Grand Valley State University, feeling like I needed the escape from small-town America. After some time, I found Grand Rapids also felt like a small town, but wrapped in a few more pretty buildings and shiny exteriors paid for by a few big families. I was still one of a few Asians I knew, and I was still looking for cultural experiences and competency from the community.

The city I live in prides itself on having the world's largest art contest, the largest urban historic districts in the US, some of the world's leading furniture design companies, and that it is the first city to have a public art piece funded by the National Endowment for the Arts (NEA). Yet our schools lack funding to sustain their art programs, or many programs for that matter.

It's not enough for the diverse range of people who reside here. Sometimes it feels like there's a fear of real authentic culture. There is culture and diversity, but mostly in pockets outside of downtown. You'll have to drive south down Division to experience more flavor and tones of brown. I have noticed in the past few years more businesses owned by people of color, and more diverse voices and educational opportunities and venues. I see and hear the many people that hunger for more, whatever their background.

The work I do now is filling the voids that made me want to leave. I'm an artist, activist, organizer, and teacher. I teach and organize to provide perspective through art and events. Sometimes I feel that if I don't do it, who will?

I wasn't allowed to talk about my life before the US, nor did I feel comfortable to or understood why while growing up. By college, expression was a struggle when it came to the artistic process. I was good at making, but connecting to concepts deeply was stood opposite to my learned culture. I was not interested in reliving traumas my classmates would not understand and being vulnerable in an educational institution that graded the validity of my lived experience. Having realized these issues years later, I found that other adults, who had similar experiences, felt similarly. Adoptees, children of immigrants, and immigrants, who also felt displaced, were defined by their appearance, despite how they identified culturally—not always being fully accepted by any side.

Artists of color.

Artists of Asian-Pacific descent.

We were one of the few students of color in our programs, and we did not have the vocabulary or know exactly what we were trying to express early on, because we had little to no examples relative to our narratives. The curriculum was not designed for our viewpoints as artists and people of color, with varied cultural, ethnic, and life experiences. The West Michigan and local communities are not always open to our viewpoints. There's a color blindness that avoids the needs and histories of individuals who don't fit the white, middle-class, Christian profile. There was a lack of diverse narratives. Whether it's elementary school or college, the Eurocentric tendencies deem some experiences as invalid. It can push individuals out who don't conform. Even in a liberal arts setting, my experiences felt like an idea. They were not considered a reality and they were approached with discomfort. The realness is scary and uncomfortable.

***

I didn't always want to be a teacher, but the more I engaged with art, the more I realized it was my vehicle for more than just creating objects. The white walls didn't always feel relatable or truly capture the depth of the art displayed and critiqued. I found more meaning in my interactions with people through art than in the process of making it, rather than constructing high-reaching concepts that aren't accessible. My first large-scale collaboration in college defined that moment for me. Designing and executing a sculptural fountain with a team, all of us with no experience, was my first taste of real stress. It had three, eight-foot-wide slabs of terra cotta concrete, with the tops mimicking the contour of the Grand River. The interior side had a bronze topographical map; the other side archived everyday objects or memorialized personal and family items in cast bronze. Water cascaded off both sides of each slab. This was on top of our regular course load. Things got tough. I stepped up.

I took on a leadership role, which surprised some. For me, doing something outside the confines of the classroom was much more relevant and motivating than class critique alone. Instead of talking about how my art could be perceived, I was engaging directly with the public. I wasn't solely in the studio, but collaborating with others to construct the product and coordinating tasks. I was inspired. However, my Asian face and some cultural behaviors were misperceived by my peers and instructors as quiet. I knew, but didn't know, how to address the unconscious and untrue bias of Asians being quiet, passive, submissive, obedient workers—meaning not leadership material. At the time I felt frustrated and defeated, especially by the end of my thesis project. That struggle shaped the way I now approach art and teaching.

Silence is not a lack of thought or strength. Silence is constantly misinterpreted, adding to implicit biases about people's abilities. It affected me.

Curating shows and teaching are ways that I have found to educate and challenge those notions. Bringing people together, building knowledge, and creating cultural opportunities has been my response to those experiences and the environment around me.

Teaching in the Grand Rapids area has given me perspective on the issues that face students and families with financial struggles, of color, and with disabilities, in contrast with those more privileged.

It is a reality, I have found, that many aren't always willing to face, because it means having to be honest with ourselves, to face our own reflections, and to see how we play a role in sustaining or changing circumstances. Accepting everyone's truth would be a first step.

For example, institutional racism is evident in the school makeup, the franchising of education, and the student response. As a person of color, who experienced marginalization in my own education, I was infuriated and saddened when students from another district knowingly flew symbols of hate as their predominantly white school played football against the predominantly black Grand Rapids school. I believe pairing a Trump banner and the Betsy Ross flag was ill-intentioned towards our African American students. This demonstration of racism was at Grand Rapids Public Schools' Houseman Field.

And there are other stories. A friend's son's school had a cafeteria incident where white students shouted "build the wall" at their Hispanic classmates.

There are folks that excuse and ignore these incidents, while others are moved to work for change and to support communities and individuals that need it. I know how I felt as a young person of color, but I can only imagine the magnitude of how our current state is impacting our kids now. Yet, despite these circumstances, I've never been so proud of the people of Grand Rapids. Having participated in some protests myself, I saw many take to the streets in numerous protests for Not My President, the Day without Immigrants, and more. I saw folks who don't typically get involved become moved to speak up, unwilling to let their neighbors stand alone. I saw former students protesting with their fellow high school friends.

It's seeing these things that move me to keep fighting and to stay.

I myself have become more and more outspoken against the values and actions I do not agree with; I refuse to be silent when I witness mistreatment or inequities and inaccuracies in education. More and more, I see that even with good intentions, power feeds only itself, and many structures are self-preserving even if they promise to serve. More and more, I realize that I needed to create my own space. I think many others feel that way too. I've committed myself to taking risks and creating new pathways in my life and in my work.

Being a member of the Avenue for the Arts, an arts organization, neighborhood, and business corridor on South Division, has been beneficial, bringing people together to challenge biases. I am finding that the art community is becoming more supportive and open than when I first felt tired of the scene. More diverse voices are featured, but we still have a ways to go. It is a start.

Opportunities such as organizing the first Asian Festival became a canvas for painting a different image of the city. It's something I can speak to from personal experience, and where I can provide the resources I hungered for but didn't have. Each of us on the committee came with our personal motivations, but we all were united in our goal of bringing awareness of Asian American cultures, heritage, and pride. I worked on coordinating performers, artists, and programming.

We worked to create a platform for voices that are not always heard, and with faces that are not always recognized as American. The diversity of Asian-Pacific Americans includes different narratives and experiences and we must give validity to their concerns in our own community.

It's also evident that there are internal struggles within Asian-Pacific American communities that many don't realize. Not all Asian-Pacific people see the same side of the rice bowl; a concept that does not occur to most, because the Asian community hasn't been very visible or understood in Grand Rapids, lumped into one non-dimensional group: model minorities with no problems.

But the concept is true for Asians, as well. We're taught to accept the blandness, like instant rice, as a form of American assimilation. This is damaging to our identities and communities. Just as there are broader calls for intersectional acceptance, we need to accept the breadth of individual identities within our complex (Asian/Asian-Pacific) community; otherwise, if we cannot lift ourselves up, it's less likely that change can be made.

Grand Rapids is our city. It's everyone's home.

We don't need to prove we're good enough.

Together we make the city better.

Planting Roots and Finding a Home through Community Engagement

by Bethany Reed

I bought my house in a run-down part of southeast Grand Rapids, Michigan, in early 2003. I was a young, single mother who also worked full-time and went to college. I was not "involved in my community." I wasn't involved in anything except my own life. I didn't really have the time. Prior to purchasing my house, I had never learned to plant the roots of community. I didn't really feel like I ever belonged anywhere.

A few years went by. My life became less complicated. I graduated from college and found a career that didn't leave me strapped for cash or on government assistance. For the first time in my life, I found myself in a position where I could look around, beyond myself and my own immediate needs.

The city, my neighborhood, and my old run-down house had started to feel like a real home to me. I had begun to settle into my community and make friends. Since I didn't really know where to begin with giving back, I looked to my friends, family, and neighbors for guidance.

At the recommendation of a few close friends, I joined a couple of women's groups such as Planned Parenthood's Justice Engagement Team (JET) and the National Organization for Women (NOW) and advocated for better sex education and better access to health care and birth control. At my mom's suggestion, I delivered food to seniors on the weekends through Area Community Services Employment and Training/Community Action Agency (ACSET/CAA). When I had the time, I gave my time. When I had extra money, I donated. It wasn't much.

What I did not expect to find through volunteering and advocacy was a sense of community and confidence that I did not have before. There is a wonderful, supportive network of people out there that really wants to make the world a better place and is willing to put in the effort. They understand that they might not be able to affect change on a global scale, but they can make their neighborhood, school, or city a better place. I learned how grassroots activism takes real work. The people who I have met and worked with have a wealth of patience and perseverance. It's truly inspiring.

A few more years went by. I worked on many home improvement projects and as my home became more beautiful inside and out, so did the area around me. The run-down street from 2003 became a charming, well-manicured neighborhood by 2012. Multi-unit buildings were converted back into single-family homes and poorly maintained houses were purchased cheap and flipped at a higher price. Young professionals were eager to move into a hip, walkable neighborhood and many were willing to pay a premium. I watched as many of my cherished neighbors were priced off my street and gentrification took its hold. My neighborhood was changing, and though many of these changes were good, it was easy to see the issues, too.

I had worked at a property management company, Urban Pharm, for about a year when I started to become concerned about my neighborhood and the surrounding community's housing issues. Everyone should have equal access to a safe, affordable place to live. It was because of my house that I could build the life I had for myself and my daughter, and I felt that stabilization began with housing. Through my job, I began to work actively with nonprofit organizations, partnering not only with housing voucher programs like Section Eight, which help mostly working women with children to afford apartments, but also Samaritas Refugee Services (formerly Lutheran Social Services), Bethany Christian Services (BCS), Refugee Services, Community Rebuilders, Youth Homelessness, and Veteran Homelessness Prevention. By working in the for-profit sector, but partnering with nonprofits, my goal was to reach as many different groups as I could. My activist identity had begun to define itself.

These days, every room in my 100-plus-year-old house has been updated and most of the big projects are now done. My child is now a teenager. I still work with Urban Pharm as their director of operations. My income is enough to comfortably support my daughter and me. Yet there is a dangerous person in charge of our country and I again find myself wanting to do more.

I'm taking my activism and volunteering to the next level. In addition to my housing advocacy through work and my reproductive rights advocacy through volunteering with Planned Parenthood, I have also joined the American Civil Liberties Union (ACLU), the Michigan Democratic Party (MDP), and have worked with Grand Rapids Racial Equity Network (GGREN). I'm attending rallies whenever I can. I'm calling my representatives about issues that matter to me. I'm showing up to town hall meetings. I'm advocating on behalf of refugees, minorities, my LGBTQ daughter and her friends, and for all of us.

As far as housing goes, I have applied to several local housing boards and hope to be considered soon. This should put me in a better position to affect change and hopefully make housing more equitable for everyone in Grand Rapids.

Over the years, my level of engagement has ebbed and flowed. Life both gets in the way and motivates action. There is no special recipe for activism, and it doesn't have to consume you for you to be able to help your community. I really feel if everyone just gave two hours a month to whatever cause they were interested in, we could change the country for the better. This could be anything. Learn how to build a house with Habitat for Humanity. Teach folks to read at your local literacy center. Distribute food to seniors through your community action agency. Volunteer to walk pets at the Humane Society. Participate in a bike race to end juvenile diabetes. Any little thing helps, and it really does make a difference. I found that by reaching out to the community that helped me, I found places to give back. Later on, I found my own voice and my own path in activism.

Yes. You will make a difference in the community by doing these things, but I am also speaking to the difference that you will see in yourself. I found that by engaging in the community even a little bit, it made me confident, inspired, and more in touch with the community. I became more interested in my neighbors. I cared more. By engaging in the community, you can find the things that matter to you. You can find your home.

Bottom-Up, Top-Down

...where we learn a variety of ways to be involved

Mary. Saint. Skunk.

by KT Herr

Lawn ornaments of the disenchanted I find
while lassoing neighbors' generosity
in the name of public media; here a tiny tulip flag,
there a flightless angel. Windmills with wings
for some fairy-dog hybrid, *Wine Much Laugh Often,*
white rabbits with red eyes—some kind of sign?

I trundle up the walk past the For Sale sign,
predict that behind an ochre door I'll find
exquisitely tousled head and crisp shirt of often-
hassled money manager, whose generosity
he wears to dinners like a pair of wings,
carried above him like his private nation's flag.

Him I'll channel when confidence flags,
when I'm eighty dollars short and need a sign
I'll still make quota—when script fails, charisma wings
it, maybe wins. Because his generation couldn't find
the compassion to birth legislation from generosity,
I quench myopia with philosophy often.

I quench my hopelessness with liquor often.
Who doesn't? Something we can all sport a yard flag
for: *Cocktail O'Clock.* But who's repping generosity?
Even the dudes who feel the Bern won't sign
up for the minimum monthly donation. Find
me a Daniel Tiger fan waiting in the wings

or an octogenarian whose attention wings
to ancient past and back again so often
he adores Antiques Roadshow but can't find
his checkbook. It's *ok, sir, yes, that is an old flag,*
we take credit cards as well—click here to sign—
I'm sure it's worth a lot; (cue smile) *as is your generosity.*

There's the rub; see, without relentless generosity
capitalism crumbles, worth melts. If wishes were wings
stout garden pigs could fly, and my friends could long since sign
leases, mortgage agreements, autographs for fans; how often
does what we salute lose white and blue, become a red flag,
become the loss we gambled we weren't born to find?

It's what I tend to find: accessories trump generosity.
Flowers sniff stiff polyester flags, but no gift here. Prove wings
abandon angels often. Give something. Give me a sign.

I wrote this piece as part of April's National Poetry Month poem-a-day challenge. To make the challenge more interesting, I put together a list of thirty poetic styles, with the goal of writing one of each throughout the month. The sestina is a fairly strict form, requiring the repetition of six line-end words in a set order. The rigidity of the form called to mind the precision of language necessary while canvassing, and the repetitive structure echoed the process of approaching door after door with the same entreaty, often receiving identical responses.

I remember being struck by how the appearance of a house would dictate my expectations, and how those expectations changed upon the opening of the door, and yet again only a few words into the conversation. What confounded me most was what people believe they can afford; to spend thirty-five dollars on a lawn ornament—or $70,000 on a brand new car—but to draw the line at five dollars a month to support a crucial public service from which they and their families directly benefit. The psychological struggle of remaining positive and combating defeatism was constant and often all-encompassing. However, the resulting bonds of friendship I established with my fellow canvassers are deep and abiding.

Balancing Justice, Charity, and Protest
by Erika C. VanDyke

Recently, someone close to me asked how I would be spending my Saturday. I replied that I would be participating in the Women's March on Washington rally taking place just a few blocks away from my home in Grand Rapids that morning, and later in the afternoon I would be working, helping a family.

In fact, I would be delivering furniture to a family at the school where I work as a family and community resource coordinator. This family had a tough year. Over the previous summer, the mom had been stopped because of her immigration status and entered deportation proceedings. While she didn't say exactly what happened, we know that somehow, she made it back to her family. She's a Latina single mom with two young kids. When she got back, she had to double up with a family member in a house that was too small for both families. She had a difficult time getting work because she doesn't speak English, and of course doesn't have papers. Finding housing was difficult for the same reasons. I've had a lot of families lately, both documented and undocumented, struggling to find housing.

According to 2015 Census data, nearly one-fifth of Michigan's immigrant population is Latinx, and 5 percent of Michigan's overall population is Latinx when including those born in the United States. Moreover, approximately 16 percent of Grand Rapids residents and 20 percent in the Grand Rapids suburb of Wyoming are Latinx. Overall, about 10 percent of Kent County residents are Latinx. Historically, immigrants have come to Michigan as agricultural workers—Michigan is the second-most agriculturally diverse state after California. Many have stayed with their families, and many continue to work in the sector, among many others.

A couple of weeks ago, we found out that another family from the school was helping by buying this family food, because there wasn't any in the house. As I contacted the mom to find out how I could help, she told me that they had finally gotten an apartment. She told me they didn't have very much furniture. I pressed for more information, and she said there were two small beds— for the children. When I asked if there was one for her, she looked away.

Part of my job is helping families like this one— finding furniture, handing mom a Meijer gift card, asking about winter clothes and kitchen supplies. Thanks to some generous partners in the community, I was able to track down a couple pieces of furniture, including a new bed. That won't come in until next week, but the couch and dresser that were donated could be delivered whenever I found someone to help me pick them up and coordinated a time with the family to drop them off. The mom to whom we would be making the delivery works all the time— Saturday is her day off, so a Saturday delivery it would be.

I can't do my job without the help of partners and volunteers, and when it comes to transporting furniture, it's part of my job to find someone with a truck and some muscle to do the heavy lifting. Luckily, we have an amazing mom who volunteers at my school. Just the other week, she offered me her truck if I ever needed it to help a family. She and her husband were willing to give up part of their Saturday afternoon to help me lift and transport the furniture to the new apartment. They did it because that's how a community works. We have to help each other.

So, to the person who asked about my weekend plans, I replied that I would be rallying in the morning, and helping a family in the afternoon. I got this response: "Rallying sounds lame, but helping families sounds good!" I can't get it out of my mind. The response says to me that, to this person, justice sounds lame, but charity sounds good. It displays a total disconnect between those two ideas. It refuses to acknowledge the link between why I felt like I needed to go out and participate in the protests, and the situation of the family I was serving.

Let me be clear, none of this is new. Families like the one described above have been living under the threat of separation because of deportation for years. President Obama deported a record number of people during his time in office, and President

Trump has vowed to make removals a priority by increasing funding for border patrol agents and changing policies around deportation priorities.

Additionally, as a woman of color, this mom faces an even larger gender-based wage gap than her white female counterparts. Indeed, 37 percent of Grand Rapids families that identify as Hispanic or Latinx live in poverty, compared to only 12 percent of white families. As housing costs continue to rise and minimum wage fails to keep up with inflation, more and more families experience homelessness. According to US Department of Housing and Urban Development reports, homelessness decreased in Michigan between 2010 and 2016, but in the Grand Rapids metro area, the number of people experiencing homelessness actually increased between 2011 and 2015. 2015 US census data showed that Grand Rapids rental availability was at less than 1 percent, the lowest in the nation. In 2016, the realty company Zillow reported that in some neighborhoods, rents rose nearly 20 percent.

Moreover, a lack of affordable daycare options in the United States mean that we had to sweet talk our (underfunded, understaffed) after-school program into accepting the kids so mom could work. Did I mention the wait list for that program was something like fifty students long? The kids that attend our school do so in overcrowded classrooms because public education funding keeps getting cut.

All of these things, and more, have been true and threaten to get worse as the current administration appoints people whose qualifications are laughable to run things like the Department of Education or Housing and Urban Development. So yes, I'll hunt down furniture for these families. I'll make sure a mom who works twelve-hour shifts has a soft place to sleep at night. I'll recruit volunteers and community partners to meet these and other needs. I'll do these things on nights and weekends and any other time I am asked to because our families deserve it.

But here's the thing. If I'm not also out there protesting and advocating and demanding better, then I'm not doing anything more than putting a Band-Aid on, or worse yet, obscuring the much bigger, systemic issues underlying the needs of the families in my community.

This isn't to say that participating in a Women's March was necessarily the correct or only way to protest or to demand better. Indeed, there are a lot of very smart, thoughtful people who had real objections to the march itself, with its lack of intersectionality, among other concerns.

But the larger point, that I'm not doing my job if I'm not both meeting immediate needs and advocating for long-term, systemic changes, stands. We must do both. If we can feel good about delivering some furniture, or dropping off some food, or donating to the cool nonprofit of the moment, then we're missing the point. We're refusing to acknowledge why those problems exist. And when we do that, everybody loses.

The Art of Quiet Leadership
by Jenny Kinne

For a long time, I did not think I was an activist. I could not match my perceptions of activism with my own reality. I thought activists were energetic, megaphone-wielding extroverts with larger-than-life personalities. I pictured speeches rousing masses, and marchers chanting in the faces of oncoming police.

I am a quiet and introspective person. I came to life as a political being in Washington, DC, where I did my best to become a revolutionary rabble-rouser, only to find that I could not fit myself into that mold. When I moved back home to Grand Rapids, Michigan, I found space for my quiet activism. Here I am learning the art of introverted leadership, and my journey has shown me that stories and long-term relationship building comprise the foundation of any successful grassroots movement. Luckily, Grand Rapids is a great place for listening and friendship.

A Big, Small Town

I think of Grand Rapids as a big, small town. Our city is growing rapidly. There is no shortage of new things to see and people to meet, but when you walk into a coffee shop, you will most likely run into someone you know. As our city grows, it is becoming more progressive. It is hard to miss the ever-increasing presence of rainbow flags and "Black Lives Matter" yard signs. Unfortunately, these shining symbols often cover up deep issues of discrimination and gentrification in our community. Still, we are a shifting people.

Grand Rapids is a midwestern city. I posit that an average midwesterner is friendly but a bit standoffish. I certainly see myself in this description. We get stuck in our own social bubbles because we fear exposure to difference, but since we are also nice, we are totally okay talking to one another.

Having lived in Washington, DC, for a few years, I am grateful for the home I have found in Grand Rapids culture. Relationships in DC often feel transactional—find out what people do and build your bubble accordingly. In Grand Rapids, my conversations usually start with something like, "How is your day?"; "Are you enjoying the sunshine?"; or "I love your garden. Did you do it yourself?" My heart has opened up to a wide variety of people in this big, small town. I am a liberal, atheist hater of athletics who has become close friends with ministers, Republicans, and yoga instructors. Grand Rapids provides ample opportunity to step outside of my bubble.

Joys and Hardships of Hanging Out

Several memories stick out as examples of how Grand Rapids has taught me to become a whole person and a political activist.

In 2010, something big happened that changed the way local organizations worked together in Grand Rapids. The Affordable Care Act passed, transforming the world of health care, and organizations had to partner with one another to understand the law and get the community enrolled. As a volunteer enrollment counselor with Planned Parenthood at the time, I set my sights on working with Bethany Christian Services Refugee Program. This was particularly important given the fact that these two organizations had never worked together. It is common in Grand Rapids a city with a large, faith-based nonprofit sector, to have tensions between faith-based and non-faith-based organizations. Building new bridges in this arena was a focus of my work at Planned Parenthood. We came together, at first nervous and skeptical, to discuss the pressing healthcare needs of immigrants and refugees in Grand Rapids.

Out of this conversation came an unlikely partnership. It became clear that we needed one another. We found a shared goal that bridged a deep divide, and we strengthened our relationship as joint education and enrollment began. We met in Bethany's space; they recruited their clients who needed health insurance and we provided our expertise in the form of trained certified application counselors. It was a wonderful example of sharing space but dividing labor and leadership roles based on expertise.

We became friends, and since this was a difficult program, we shared joyful ups and heartbreaking downs. We faced technological challenges when the health care website would break down or computers wouldn't work. We faced language barriers, having to arrange for translation for refugees who spoke rare languages and facing the task of explaining complicated processes in multiple languages. Most devastatingly, though, were the cases where the system itself was not built to cope with the unique challenges faced by these people and we had to turn them away or delay getting them the help that they needed. Despite all of these challenges, each time one of our certified application counselors successfully enrolled a family in the health insurance program, we celebrated the accomplishment of a shared mission and felt deeply the impact that we were having on the lives of the people we were working with. We got to know over 100 people during enrollment, and their stories and friendships kept us going, challenging us to keep breaking down barriers.

Taking the time to listen and share stories builds political power. On a night shortly after the Planned Parenthood shooting in Colorado on November 27, 2015, I invited a group of Planned Parenthood and Black Lives Matter volunteers to my home. This was a difficult and personal conversation that did not need to happen in public. We came to my living room already knowing and trusting one another, but we also came very explicitly as community leaders who wanted to create change in local work and conversation. We sat in my little living room and talked for a couple of hours, delving into our dreams and nightmares as controversial activists. For a blip of time, my living room felt like a sanctuary floating above the world's daily violence.

Of course, the world keeps spinning. Racism persists. Attacks on reproductive health care persist. I am humbled to be a part of these conversations, but they certainly are not enough. Conversations must eventually move toward action, but we have to start by slowing down and talking to one another. We need to hang out more.

Hanging out isn't always a love-filled dreamscape. Sometimes, hanging out means you are going to be called out on your shit. As a board member of the Grand Rapids chapter of the National Organization for Women, we invited a renowned racial justice advocate, Chaka Holley, to be a part of our annual fundraiser. Chaka blew us all away with her intelligence, kindness, and sense of humor. What I admire most about Chaka is her ability to speak hard truth in a way that opens up paths to friendship and hope. She called out the feminist community of Grand Rapids for failing to prioritize racial equity and inclusion within our organizations. This hurt for a lot of people in my feminist community, and we had many conversations about how to listen. Chaka gave us information that was necessary but hard to hear, so we needed to train our hearts to pay attention and objectively look at solutions posed, rather than getting defensive. These conversations made us better people and activists. Listening and hanging out isn't always easy, but I think it pays off every time.

Sit Down, Shut Up, and Listen

With all that said, hanging out is not enough. We have to hang out and listen to one another. We miss too much when we are busy talking. We miss thoughts, values, and experiences that have shaped our friends and neighbors. We will neither understand fault lines nor build bridges without deep listening.

I learned to listen through a project that I ran with Planned Parenthood. We realized that facts and figures are not what are changing the hearts and minds of people, most especially the people in positions to make decisions about reproductive issues. Facts and figures get thrown into the world, but the context and the meaning is too often left up to interpretation. Facts and figures have no faces. While I worked for a large nonprofit organization, I knew that a more grassroots, people-centered approach was needed in order for us to bring that meaning and context into our activist work. We created an online platform where people could securely share their stories and protocol for how we could sensitively interview people and collect their stories. This became the 100 Stories for 100 Years program at Planned Parenthood of Michigan to celebrate the centennial anniversary of the organization.

What was interesting is that the stories were already there. The people who are Planned Parenthood patients and activists all have stories and share them on a regular basis. We just hadn't been listening. It was important to me to let those stories guide our work, to let the people for whom our services and our advocacy was important be the ones who told us what work needed to be, rather than a more traditional, prescriptive form of organizing. It was time for us to shut up and listen.

We, as an organization, learned a lot. I learned a lot. I learned that sharing stories requires trust and can never be a transactional. Instead, it is transformative. It cannot simply be a goal-oriented tactic to be used by organizations. It is about relationship building. It is about reflection, bonding, and opening yourself to the experiences of others. You cannot use people for their stories. The stories must stand on their own with people being allowed to express their experiences in ways that are authentic and that showcase the voice of the storyteller.

During this project, I learned the importance of shutting up and listening. My own assumptions were often challenged, and I learned to become comfortable with those challenges. I learned that stories can create community—whether in person at storytelling events or online through social media. People relate to stories.

These formative experiences have taught me that successful activism requires us to sit down, shut up, and listen. We certainly need eloquent and extroverted leaders in our movements for social change, but we also need quiet movers and shakers. We need to value our listeners and storytellers in the same way we do our tireless figureheads. Activists who take the time to rest and form relationships through asking questions are pivotal to sustainable grassroots movements.

Forming relationships and sharing stories builds bridges and cultivates political power. I feel lucky to have learned this at a young age, and I look forward to a lifetime of introverted activism. After a long time of trying to fit myself into an activism mold that didn't fit, I am proud to finally embrace my personality. I am quiet. I am a listener. I am a leader.

Fostering Student Activism

by Julia M. Mason and Kathleen Underwood

This piece was written in consultation with Jo Ann Wassenaar and Marlene Kowalski-Braun.

Over a decade, we—Julia Mason, Kathleen Underwood, and Jo Ann Wassenaar—had the opportunity to work with more than 100 students, most of them minors or majors in Women and Gender Studies (now Women, Gender, and Sexuality Studies) who were and are deeply committed to bringing feminist theory to activism. In two courses, the "Women's Community Collaborative" (WCC) and "Contemporary Theory and Practicum," we guided students to identify social justice issues they were passionate about, design projects that addressed those issues, and make significant steps toward solving the issues. Women and Gender Studies (WGS) faculty members Kathleen and Julia provided the course structures and Jo Ann worked with each student to find relevant internships and/or obtain support for projects. Such collaboration did not develop without two important ingredients: a great deal of planning and a deeply held belief that modeling feminist practice was essential. Indeed, feminist practice was the foundational ideal for the "Women's Community Collaborative" as originally outlined in 2005 by Marlene Kowalski-Braun, then Director of the Grand Valley State University Women's Center.

The courses grew out of and were designed to foster a feminist commitment to connecting theory and practice. This meant a collaborative relationship between WGS and the Women's Center. Research and theory about community engagement were present in the course readings and assignments but they also underpinned the entire structure of the class. Feminist leadership is attentive to power dynamics, addresses intersectional issues, and is committed to moving beyond individual empowerment to creating and supporting systemic change. We focused on guiding students in developing practical and philosophical approaches to leadership.

From the outset, the "Women's Community Collaborative" combined an internship with coursework, readings, and discussions on activism and social change, so that students might examine and analyze the theoretical underpinnings of injustice while working to create social change. The internships, mostly women-centered and all with nonprofits in the greater Grand Rapids area, varied widely; yet we encouraged students to find commonality in the work. A key component of the class was an organizational needs assessment that interns carried out, which helped them identify ways to support their specific agency. Drawing on what they learned, students worked independently or in groups to develop tools. Some designed social media campaigns, while others developed curriculum. Many were involved in the fundraising activities of their nonprofits, including event support, administrative tasks, and research. These various activities allowed students to hone their skills, work in a professional environment, and develop a better understanding of the full range of work in the nonprofit sector. For some, the WCC experience helped them decide if working in a nonprofit was in their future.

Designed as a culminating course for WGS minors, "Contemporary Theory and Practicum" (WGS 491), encouraged students to put theory into action. Drawing on work done in their "Feminist Theory" class, they were able to: 1) describe the problem they were concerned about, 2) analyze why that problem exists, 3) imagine a world in which the problem had been solved, and 4) strategize actions that might lead to solving the problem. Becoming aware that there might be a wide range of possible actions, all directed at similar problems, was significant because it allows for a range of solutions and potential collaborations. Take for example, sexual assault, a topic that was addressed in every WGS 491 class that Kathleen taught. One group of students raised money to bring in a national educational speaker; another student designed a pub mat with information to raise awareness about date rape drugs; other students worked as interns in the Women's Center to facilitate sexual assault programming (e.g., Take Back the Night, Silent Witness, and Rock Against Rape).

Another problem that students addressed was the feminization of poverty. Students in different semesters raised funds to provide feminine hygiene products to homeless women.

Both WGS 491 and WCC provided students space to put theory into action; however, feminist activism is now woven throughout WGS, beginning with a brief project in the "Introduction to Gender Studies" course, and followed by a more rigorous discussion of theory and action in "Feminist Theory". A recent curriculum revision now requires WGS majors to engage in an activist-related project by completing one of several options. In this essay, however, we focus on the "Women's Community Collaborative" because it:

- Provides insights into the collaboration necessary to develop and sustain the course;

- Pays attention to several alums of this course who have found positions of social change leadership in Grand Rapids;

- Reveals how networks can be developed among nonprofit leaders and activists.

Collaborations

At every step, the course was scaffolded on collaboration. The course had its origins in a strong commitment to providing a dynamic and connected curricular and co-curricular experience for students. Additionally, as the result of a Women's Center grant, Marlene saw a way to provide funds for students who would intern in women-centered nonprofits in the greater Grand Rapids region; Kathleen strategized about how to add a classroom component to an internship; Jo Ann drew on her close connections to the nonprofits in the region to secure internships; and Julia created the curriculum that would help students see connections between what they were learning and what they were doing. From the outset, we designed the Women's Community Collaborative as reciprocal, benefiting both the student interns and the agencies. Jo Ann and Julia interviewed prospective interns to be sure each one understood the ways in which a WCC internship differed from other internships, especially the theoretical component. The coursework, including readings and discussions, focused on strategies for collaboration as individuals and among agencies. Students grappled with some of the challenges of balancing day-to-day tasks and long-term strategic activist strategies. The realities of the nonprofit landscape in West Michigan included economic, philosophic, and logistical challenges, as well.

Many of the initial agencies were already partners with the Women's Center and WGS, and Jo Ann met with the individual supervisors to determine the agency needs and to clarify the specific internship requirements and tasks. It was important to make sure that intern placements would serve the needs of the agencies while supporting student development. The nonprofit sector in West Michigan presented challenges and opportunities. During the initial decade of the WCC, Michigan preceded the rest of the nation in an economic downturn, which meant a shifting landscape for nonprofit agencies. Many faced contractions of staff, the elimination of positions, and the revision of missions because of the local and national economic situation.

While all agencies have different needs regarding kinds of work and placements, Jo Ann took great care to ensure that interns would be involved in meaningful activities including taking ownership of projects as appropriate, and she was intentional in placing interns. As the course developed, we determined that interns needed more preparation to take on their responsibilities, and Jo Ann implemented a training that included a panel of past interns and supervisors. Over that first decade, students found internships at such organizations as the Center for Women in Transition, YWCA West Central Michigan, Kids' Food Basket, the Grand Rapids Red Project, Planned Parenthood, Women's Resource Center, Grand Rapids Opportunities for Women, Girl Scouts of Michigan Shore to Shore, and Safe Haven Ministries.

A central component of the course was for students to understand that, while each nonprofit has a specific mission and projects, there were challenges that confronted all of them. Initially, we asked students to identify the common issues across their sponsoring agencies and to work collectively to find solutions that they might present to those agencies. This assignment required students come to a consensus about what to present and how. They showcased their solution at the end of the semester at an agency wrap-up that also served as an opportunity for reflection, for recognition of the work completed, and for fostering continued partnerships. Some cohorts used the agency wrap-up as an opportunity to model and/or make explicit missed or new opportunities for inter-agency collaboration. Activism, as a student intern learned, can take many forms: implementing new programs, revising existing programs to be more inclusive and more sustainable, and expanding definitions of justice.

Former Students, Current Leaders

Preparing the next generation of feminist nonprofit leaders was always a goal for the WCC, and it has been rewarding for us to reflect on what our alums are doing. Several have gone on to rewarding jobs in the public sector as program directors and counselors, and others have obtained professional degrees, including law, social work, medicine, higher education leadership, and in academe. What has been particularly gratifying is to know that several of our former students have found ways to sustain their commitment to feminist activism with work in organizations in West Michigan.

For this essay, we reached out to four of these students to find out what they are currently doing, and ask their assessment of the value of work they did in their final semesters at GVSU. They are Callista Cook (Employment Specialist, Goodwill Industries), Rachael Hamilton (VIPKID and counselor, Heritage Clinic for Women), Julia Raap (Youth Coordinator, Prevention and Empowerment Services, YWCA West Central Michigan), and Dani

Vilella (Advocacy and Political Field Manager, Planned Parenthood of Michigan). We requested that they reflect on the ways in which they have (or have not) been able to apply the theoretical knowledge and the practical knowledge gained in the WGS Program in their work and what role their experience with the "Women's Community Collaborative" plays (if any) in their current work. Another question asked about any social justice work outside the workplace. The final question focused on whether (or not) they were aware of the underlying collaboration that shaped the "Women's Community Collaborative." Several general themes emerged from the questions we posed:

- Connection and understanding with others and across differences;

- Theory for developing their own feminist leadership style and practical tools;

- Space to identify a feminist theoretical framework, to reflect and process, and to learn perspectives;

- Sustaining feminist practice.

Connection and Understanding with Others and Across Differences

Developing skills to connect and understand others was a theme that ran through the responses we got, and such skills are essential in the work they do. Dani's work is almost entirely with women whose backgrounds and experiences vary widely. Rachael wrote about the ways in which WCC/WGS provided her with tools to become more "empathetic" with the people she encounters, and thereby play a "more impactful role in the lives of others." Callista stated, "I work with a very diverse population, and it is important to be able to approach a situation with both empathy and knowledge."

Theory for Developing Their Own Feminist Leadership Style and Practical Tools

The reflections indicated that the readings and discussions fostered a more complex understanding of feminism(s) and how to apply them as an activist. For Dani, this meant: "I studied 'feminisms,' coming to understand the debates within feminism and the different approaches to thinking about issues that would allow me to be better able to communicate with a variety of women from different backgrounds. I learned all of the theory that lets me break down and explain the history behind and connectivity within different issues affecting women." Additionally, Julia found that the readings and discussions "introduced me to the concepts of feminist leadership and transformational leadership, which have been very influential to my perspective and the ways that I interact with my students." The 2005 book, *Grassroots: A Field Guide to Feminist Activism*, by Jennifer Baumgardner and Amy Richards played a central role in developing personal leadership. As Dani articulated, Grassroots "made activism so approachable that I came to understand myself and my role as one based in feminist activism...and shift[ed] my path toward intentional, local action."

All respondents mentioned specific, practical tools that were developed or strengthened as a result of the course and internship, as summarized by Julia: "My entire perspective has been shaped by the theoretical and practical knowledge that I gained through WGS and I utilize these tools every day." Dani echoed Julia's assessment and included several concrete examples: "I learned the realities of working in a service-based nonprofit organization. I came to understand program implementation, fundraising, and challenges of providing reliable services." Additionally, as Callista explained, the WCC "allowed an opportunity to learn about local resources, connect with professionals in the field, and gain face-to-face time with individuals I desired to serve."

Space To Identify a Feminist Theoretical Framework, To Reflect and Process, and To Learn Perspectives

Space, as both a construct of place and time, was significant for students and continues to be in their work. For Rachael, having a "space that facilitated and valued bringing ideas to term" was essential in her development and helped her acknowledge the "value" of her work. For Julia, the WCC "provided space to process and reflect," and she now incorporates space in her own classrooms where she works to establish "'brave' spaces where students feel like they can engage [challenging] topics and ideas."

Former students and current leaders discussed the ways in which the WGS courses they took provided them "lenses" or "perspectives" to view and review social issues. Rachael also articulated the ways these lenses and perspectives influence her work, providing her "uniquely well-rounded perspective on social issues." Julia articulated the thoughts of others when she discussed the necessity for a fluidity in "navigating" her work as shifting social forces have impacts on who she serves. Former students, like Callista, also found that their WGS experience taught them "to look deeper at and challenge privilege and inequality within our communities."

Sustaining Feminist Practice

Former students commented about the "costs" of nonprofit work, both financially and emotionally. Rachael noted that "being in fields that are traditionally women's work and traditionally undervalued, often with expectations to be okay with low wages and working off the clock, I have more self-confidence to see value in myself and my work, and to expect others to see the same and act accordingly." The demands of social justice work also has emotional costs. Dani pointed out that "direct service is an emotionally draining job that is not right for everyone." Rachael echoed that point, stating she, "found local activism to be pretty emotionally draining." Julia was more succinct: "burnout is a real thing."

This frank assessment has strengthened these alums' commitment to activism as demonstrated in their feminist mentoring of the next generation. Three of our respondents (Dani, Julia, and Callista) have mentored WCC interns in subsequent years, enthusiastically attending the annual wrap-up. Julia noted that she "appreciates" the interns who work with her, and, drawing on her own experience, reported she has a clear understanding of the "struggle of managing the demands of an internship and a full course load."

Conclusions

Grassroots activism takes many forms, and for us the central theme that emerged is that "Women's Community Collaborative" provided "space" for a cohort of young feminists to develop important skills for negotiating social justice issues beyond the campus and to develop networks of support essential to the work. Modeling feminist social justice activism has been challenging and rewarding for us. In designing and implementing the course, we had to figure out how to collaborate, delegate, and trust each other. These lessons became woven into the fabric of the "Women's Community Collaborative." As with many grassroots activist strategies, there are elements that have been successful and others that have been modified over time as a result of assessment and reflection. From the beginning, it was important to select readings that illustrate many challenges, opportunities, and strategies other feminists have negotiated. Course discussions, activities, and exercises allowed space to practice, struggle together, and support each other. Internships provided practical experience, networking opportunities, and direct community engagement.

The social and political landscape of West Michigan had an impact on the course, both directly and indirectly. Students, faculty, staff, and community partners had to negotiate advocating for feminist social justice effectively in a setting that can be hostile to feminist practices. This served to strengthen resolve, inspire creativity, and foster networking. During a time of limited resources, it can be challenging to address both immediate and long term needs. Strategic choices were made about how best to meet the goals of supporting the students and community partners.

Some elements of this experience are unique to the "Women's Community Collaborative," but many lessons are applicable to all forms of social justice activism. Building sustainable partnerships is difficult, time consuming, and necessary. Taking time to learn through listening and reading is essential. Meeting people where they are and finding common ground will take time and effort but it is worth it. Activists need to be strategic, have both short- and long-term goals, and practice self-care. Progress is measured both through the impact on individuals and the communities we serve. Reflecting on the first decade of the "Women's Community Collaborative," and writing this essay, has allowed us to reminiscence on the ways that feminist teaching is always grassroots activism.

Grand Rapids: Growing Good Works from the Ground Up

by Mary Reed Kelly

Grand Rapids, like a younger sibling, has had its share of nicknames: Furniture City, River City, Beer City, and even Happy Rapids or Bland Rapids. But the state's second largest city is the primary cultural and business hub of West Michigan and has boasted impressive growth and prosperity throughout the past couple of decades. In fact, Grand Rapids and its surrounding areas are the fastest-growing population center in Michigan, according to the US Census Bureau. Citizens of Grand Rapids have been heard to claim it as one of the happiest, safest, friendliest, most hard-working places on the planet, and cite recent appearances in national media such as US News and World Report, Lonely Planet, Forbes, and the Today Show that confirm that image.

And, living here, we see some positive results from that optimism and confidence. There are Michigan communities that have suffered economic decline, urban blight, or public health crises, for instance, as Grand Rapids has been moving and shaking. Many here are working hard to welcome and embrace diverse populations, to host a broader array of arts and cultural experiences, and to woo the world's best and most prolific innovators in technology, science, and medicine—all this, while preserving and promoting Grand Rapids's longtime standing as a leader in the design and manufacturing of furniture.

This movement and enhanced profile may be because of striking publicity campaigns, beautiful beaches, historic and affordable housing, or the eight colleges located in and around Grand Rapids. More specifically, Grand Rapids is the home of ArtPrize, the annual international art competition and festival that has now been recognized as the most-attended art event on the planet. There is a lot to celebrate.

But there is still much work to be done. There still exists a contrast between the outward public appearance and the real, on-the-ground, lived experiences of many Grand Rapids residents. This is most evident in the fact that government, business, and nonprofit leadership in Grand Rapids remains predominantly white, despite a vibrantly diverse community. Thankfully, Grand Rapids has a strong network of citizen volunteers and activists pushing for open doors and open minds to enrich our city with new and challenging perspectives to bring all voices to the table and address concerns of underrepresented populations. Much of this change has been driven by tireless and often little-recognized grassroots efforts by ordinary people who want to ensure all voices are heard.

Partners in Power

But this story is not just about Grand Rapids—it's also about the people who make change in Grand Rapids. And in particular, about two women who have it made their mission, wherever and in the midst of whatever movement they find themselves, to help more people to recognize and embrace their own power to create change. Where you find your power and how you claim it is critical, for it can't be given, only realized in oneself.

Shannon Garrett grew up in an open and welcoming family of helpers who jumped in when there was a need in their small, rural Michigan community. When the paper products plant where her grandmother worked went on strike, she was a toddler, but she accompanied her mother to bring chili and coffee to friends on the picket line. After college, she did a tour in Washington, DC, trying to learn how to take those instincts to help people fight for their rights to the political arena.

She moved back to Michigan in 2007 to open a Grand Rapids office of the White House Project, a nonprofit working to increase female representation in American institutions, businesses, and government. When the challenging economic climate forced the White House Project to close its doors, Shannon started her own firm, SMG Strategies. At SMG, she works throughout West Michigan and across the country to help current and aspiring political leaders, nonprofits, and others embrace their political ambition and strengthen their civic leadership.

In 2014, Shannon and other former colleagues from the White House Project agreed there was still a need for nonpartisan political leadership training specific to women, to address obstacles and to articulate opportunities, particularly for young women and women of color. So they launched VoteRunLead, a nonprofit to recruit and train women to run for office, focusing exclusively on races at the state and local level. Following the 2016 presidential election, over 7,000 women from around the country signed up with VoteRunLead to learn how to run for office.

Meanwhile, Tera Wozniak Qualls was fairly immersed in grassroots activism in Grand Rapids as well. Tera also came from an activist family, hearing stories of her mother's and grandmother's histories in the fight for social justice. She says she was an outlier, knew she didn't fit in, and felt compelled to work against that, to use the privileges she did have to advance civil rights for all. Tera fantasized about a political future, and first went after a pageant title as a way to prove to herself that she could have affirmation, a voice, and power. She won, but realized it was probably more effective, and certainly more fulfilling, to make a difference locally, to use that power through community government, rather than through celebrity.

In 2006, she brought her power to the fight against Proposal Two, a ballot initiative aiming to eliminate Affirmative Action in Michigan. She'd been working at the Heart of West Michigan United Way and found colleagues were participating in the statewide effort, so she jumped in. The language on the ballot was very confusing and was compounded by the racial and sexist tension surrounding the initiative. Tera worked to educate voters, explain the issue, and clarify the true intent of the proposal. Sadly, her work ended when the proposal passed.

Tera's work on Proposal Two got her excited about local voter engagement, so her next move came the following year when she started with the Grand Rapids League of Women Voters and served three years as vice president, helping to lead efforts to engage voters in school board elections. The group held candidate forums, created voter guides, and knocked on doors to get voters' attention and urge them to action.

About the time she was getting involved with the League, Tera started a Grand Rapids chapter of the Young Nonprofit Professionals Network, a national movement. She did research on the needs of young professionals in the nonprofit sector and what they hoped for in their careers. Tera led the YNPN board until 2011, when she felt that a new group of young professionals should have a chance to shape the network for themselves. The local chapter is now a flourishing organization of over 200 members.

The two powerbrokers' paths intersected in 2015 when Shannon was teaching a Master's level advocacy course and realized many of her students didn't understand the basics of their local government structures. The pushes for activism seemed to always be at the national level. Tera was working in her own firm, Momentum for Impact, with several nonprofit leaders on their needs and work in the community. Both women were concerned with the lack of diversity in local government and gaps in leadership for people of color and women. Together, they created Civicize.Me, an example of social entrepreneurship that supports grassroots efforts. Civicize.Me is a place-based leadership certification program, offering a variety of courses to help local residents understand, among other things, county governments, the differences between cities, townships, villages, and how a school board differs from the city government.

The Interview

I asked Shannon and Tera about their work and what compels them to keep pushing for grassroots movement and change in Grand Rapids. Shannon says she feels a calling—not religious, but a deep drive within her to work ceaselessly until each of us knows our power. She lives off the vibe of seeing people identify and embrace their own political power. Tera used to think she needed to run for office, but has found that she can make a difference by working locally to support this ambition in others—in particular, among people in the populations least represented in elected leadership. Both Shannon and Tera agree that great progress will come, and will come faster, when local policy decisions include the experiences, expertise, and voices of more local residents, especially from people of color, women, LGBTQ people, and residents with disabilities.

What does grassroots activism look like in Grand Rapids? And how has it changed in recent years?

Tera: Activism in Grand Rapids has grown in the last decade, but it seems to be dominated by the very liberal or the very conservative, and nothing in between. There have been small activist groups around specific issues, such as animal rights and LGBTQ rights since the 1960s.

Shannon: One of the best examples in recent history of a grassroots effort here showing real results was when the Progressive Women's Alliance, a non-partisan political action committee, was formed. A direct line can be drawn from PWA's formation [in 2004] as a PAC supporting progressive women running for office to Grand Rapids getting its first woman mayor, Rosalynn Bliss in 2016, and its first African American woman, Senita Lenear, elected to the city commission in 2013. Admittedly, this was not traditional grassroots work, but it presented an opportunity for like-minded people to mobilize around a specific goal to increase representation in leadership.

Tera: We dissolved the League of Women Voters after only a couple of years of attempting a rejuvenation in local elections. Local activists seemed focused on working for change toward specific goals, like PROACTIVE [a non-partisan organization focusing on voter registration and GOTV, particularly within populations of color] and the Progressive Women's Alliance, and there was little need for another voter participation group.

Now the League of Women Voters is trying again to organize at a time when more residents across the race and political spectrum are tuned into the need to protect voters' rights and access to ballots for all.

Shannon: Grand Rapids, like West Michigan, is very segregated. In large part because of the systemic racism and unconscious bias that this segregation fosters, activist populations started to become more insulated, each working on their own focus, as opposed to in broader coalitions. But it's changing, there are more young people, more activities, events, and causes to plug into, like Grand Rapids Young Professionals, BL2END [a group providing young professionals of color with opportunities for networking and community engagement], Young Nonprofit Professionals Network, and Equity PAC [a political action committee with the mission to increase the number of equity-minded officials, policies, and practices in Michigan]. But there's still a need for spaces where people of similar backgrounds organize their own power. I'm thinking in particular of groups like Latina Network of West Michigan, formed in 2014, and Black Women Connect GR, started the following year. Successful grassroots activism needs both spaces where people from marginalized groups can build organizing strength in their own right, and spaces where people can build coalitions and movements across our divides and support a common vision.

Tera: We also see that while the city of Grand Rapids has become somewhat liberal, change has not come to the surrounding communities, especially as far as voting and policies are concerned. The money and businesses in this area are still pretty conservative.

Shannon: There are also a number of nonprofits and direct service providers working to help folks left behind in the region's and state's economic and social policy decisions. There are people on the ground trying to build grassroots movements, but a lot of the money funding these nonprofits comes from primarily conservative donors.

Tera: Yes, and that means a lot of those nonprofits will avoid some political and policy advocacy efforts because their significant donors don't believe in or don't support those efforts.

So why should people be engaged in grassroots efforts in Grand Rapids?

Shannon: It may feel like there's not a lot you can do about the president or governor or influencing national or state policy agendas, but there is definitely a lot you can do about where your money is going and how policy is determined in regard to local issues. And that work can be done proactively. You shouldn't have to wait for something horrible to happen to realize that you do have a voice in local government. Talk to your neighbors, reach outside your immediate circles to gain diverse perspectives, listen—really listen—to the voices of people who experience a life in Grand Rapids that is different than yours. And use your own power to push local governments to act accordingly. Show up to county commission meetings, make a statement during public comment periods, meet one-on-one with elected officials, invite policymakers to your events and actions. Because it is education and pressure from local voters and taxpayers that move local electeds. In particular, white people in Grand Rapids need to step back and follow the rising leadership from within communities of color. Because that's where true change and progress will come from.

Tera: Look at what you don't like. Lean back into what you know is right. And listen to your body. Your body knows when something doesn't feel right to you. It knows when you feel compelled to act, to learn, to make change. Find spaces right in your backyard that teach and help you grow.

What are the opportunities and challenges in grassroots work in Grand Rapids now?

Shannon: There's a lot of opportunity now, lots of new activism and new money to support those causes. It's not all just the traditional Christian conservative base of donor pools that's been here for so long. People of all backgrounds are using their voices and leadership to spotlight critical issues—issues like the racial outcomes of Grand Rapids's booming housing and development markets, how the changing job market does not actually employ the talents or build the skills of the local low-income populations, or why the lack of representative diversity and adequate bias training results in more racial profiling among local law enforcement.

Tera: But it can also be a challenge when people are starting new efforts in silos, instead of connecting to or being embraced by organizations already here. When efforts and groups overlap in focus but operate independently, it results in dilution of efforts and money. At the same time, you can see why people do it if they don't have the space they need or they can't get heard within existing organizations.

Shannon: That's so true. People in power—both in government and in activist groups—don't always do a good job of deliberately looking to diversify. They talk about it, and they look around the room they're in and they see the same Latina women, for example, and appoint them to everything. That's why groups like the Latina Women's Network need to exist. They are trying to expand the leadership of more Latinas and amplify their visibility in the rooms where power resides. But until the city can address this problem at the top, until the executive suites of the businesses and nonprofits follow the lead of groups like the Latina Women's Network, this won't change

Tera: It's happening across the board. We have the Grand Rapids Area Chamber of Commerce, the Grand Rapids Black

Chamber of Commerce, and the West Michigan Hispanic Chamber of Commerce in Grand Rapids. But the major power structures are all white. We have a woman mayor who comes out against racial bias and the police hire all white officers again. People of color and women of all races and ethnicities are still not getting the visibility they need. There are major systemic race issues embedded in our city's politics that need to be dismantled. This work takes time and effort that many groups are working towards currently. In the meantime, the only way for many demographic groups—"people who are drawn together by something that they have in common that has both personal and community consequences, and grant themselves the authority to solve the problem they are facing or create the future they desire"—in our city to be heard is to organize on their own, to share their own resources, and support one another.

Shannon: To be clear, Tera and I can't sit here as white, cis-gendered women and pretend to know all the challenges and opportunities facing every Grand Rapidian. And we can't act like we have all the answers. It should be obvious that we will never know what it's like to live and work and raise a family as a black woman, or a trans woman, or a woman with disabilities, in Grand Rapids. It's disturbing that there are still an untold number of local white leaders who attempt to speak on behalf of people whose lived experiences they don't understand. What Tera and I can and try to do is use our own experiences, our own expertise and knowledge, and our own privileges to assist others as they attempt to navigate the local political systems. That's what Civicize.Me is all about. It's introducing people to their backyard civic institutions—a level of government we're never taught about in school—demystifying local decision-making processes and spotlighting the opportunities and avenues to influence those decisions. We don't define or judge an individual participant's civic ambition. We believe one solution to dismantling systemic racism and accelerating true progressive change lies in amplifying the voices and efforts of the people who live under the decisions of local governments but who don't currently have a seat at the decision-making table.

What skills or characteristics are important for activism?

Tera: In the book Bowling Alone, Robert Putnam describes how all the civic organizations were disappearing, becoming more independent and individualized. So people with power, often of privilege, created organizations that they thought were important and there were no more grassroots groups. We can feel that now in Grand Rapids and in response, new organizations are cropping up and competing with these established structures. They have to compete. They need to support and lift up individuals in their own demographic groups, in order to be seen and heard by the organizations established in a traditional, white, conservative space.

Shannon: Listening is the most important activist skill. A conscious or unconscious refusal to listen is why most grassroots movements often stall. People—especially white people—come in and think they know the solution and speak on behalf of communities instead of asking them, instead of inviting them to the conversation and actually listening to their ideas and following their lead. Our Civicize.Me program is not about advancing causes, it's about equipping people to achieve whatever their cause is, to organize for change in their neighborhoods. We're not prescribing, we're just unlocking the tools to work for the change you want.

Tera: Yes, listening and really hearing. Listening and asking questions and then doing something with what you hear. There has to be more listening, and also more risk-taking in approaches to doing things that are different. There's a lack of understanding of the challenges, particularly in white-dominated leadership, an often misinformed perspective on the concerns preventing people from doing activism. There needs to be an openness to other ways of approaching activism.

What about Grand Rapids do you see in the future as helping to sustain or progress your vision?

Shannon: The 2016 election affected lots of people in lots of ways. That's evident in Grand Rapids as in other places. More people are willing to be active, to stand up and do things. The challenges will be bringing people together under a common vision, but these are the growing pains of a growing city. There's new development, new businesses, all new interests, at the same time as everyday folks in neighborhoods are finding ways to engage more intentionally and more fully.

Tera: With Schools of Choice, neighborhood kids don't necessarily go to school together anymore—families can live for years on the same street and not interact or understand the concerns of their neighbors. As a result, we've lost a sense of neighborhood community. Activism is starting to come back through neighborhood associations. From the top down, there's a sense of community pride but it's often still paternalistic. There's also lots of philanthropy to address outcomes, but they may not actually address the problem.

Shannon: There's charity and support but little investigation of why do we need this? What are the root causes that lead to us needing these types of charities and direct services?

Tera: There are huge research efforts and evaluation to find out how to fix something. For instance, philanthropy helped put in after-school programs and programs for parents through Grand Rapids public schools, but they're not necessarily addressing large-scale issues that might be impeding parents' moving out of tough situations or choosing schools that better meet their kids' needs. The issues are deeper than "bad parenting" or one "bad school." Our issues in Grand Rapids can be attributed to structural racism from decades and decades of segregation and bias in all areas of government and businesses. All indicators of success—i.e., school achievement, housing, jobs, etc.—have an overlying gap along racial lines. Black and brown people are simply being left behind because of the structures built within our city, starting so many decades ago. Fixes aren't easy. In my opinion, and I think others share this as well, some of the fixes grant-makers are making on the ground in neighborhoods will never be successful until they focus on dismantling structural racism in our city.

Shannon: Yes, that's the only way Grand Rapids will truly achieve sustainable progress.

What advice do you have for those who want to get involved?

Shannon: We're at a crossroads in Grand Rapids history—a pivotal time of critical conversations about serious political, economic, and social issues. We will come out better on the other side only as long as we can expand and retain diversity in leadership and talent throughout West Michigan, and not get so combative that people give up or leave. There are people that have stepped out, willing to take risks and fight for change. We, particularly we white folks, need to continue to stand behind these leaders and support their visions.

My advice for people is to "just do it." Don't wait for others to authorize you. There's no magic council that bestows the title of "expert" or "leader" on you. We need to authorize each other to speak our truths, and then honor and validate those truths. The levers for change are there; don't hesitate to ask for help accessing them. We'll all do better when we communicate more.

Tera: I'd mention the importance of networking and coalition building. Know people and know how to get them on your side. Lean into what you know is right. Listen to that, get engaged. If you feel powerless, tap into your network to find others who can help renew your energy and plug you into the right avenues for change.

Thanks very much for your time and inspiration, Tera and Shannon.

In talking with Tera and Shannon, one feels hope and optimism, tempered with apprehension about all that still needs to be done. Grand Rapids is growing from a small town into a significant city. It's flexing its capabilities and its outlook in diversity, in the arts, in education, and in business. As with any organism, growth often means pain and challenges, but it offers opportunities and enticement to jump in and take a stand, to help move a cause forward, or to get a candidate elected, to build on those successes.

But it's important to remember that success in activism takes different forms. It's a success when a candidate is elected, but it's also a type of success even if that candidate loses a race. There's power in being able to hold the opposition accountable for answering questions that might not have come up, for speaking to issues that might not have been raised. And it empowers others, those who are observing, who've not yet taken their steps toward activism. It gives them the courage and the knowledge that they can play a role in bringing issues to light and in making positive change in their neighborhoods or in their communities.

We hope you'll take note of the grassroots work that's happening in Michigan's second biggest city. It's good for Grand Rapids and it's good for all of us. The Saguaro Seminar for Civic Engagement in America at Harvard Kennedy School calls civic engagement and volunteering "the new hybrid health club for the twenty-first century that's free to join and miraculously improves both your health and the community's through the work performed and the social ties built." Join Tera and Shannon and the countless current movements to keep Grand Rapids vibrant, healthy, and successful for all its residents.

LadyfestGR: Grassroots Fundraising for Grassroots Nonprofits

by Jes Kramer

As a female musician playing shows in venues all around Michigan, I have experienced many instances of micro-aggressions and condescending language from men. From the assumption that I'm not the one actually playing the instruments I'm loading in to blatantly ignoring requests for how my sound should be mixed, these issues come from venue staff as well as attendees. The under-representation of women in live music is obvious if you walk into any handful of shows in this city. Conversations with musicians and booking agents from around the country confirm that this problem is not specific to Grand Rapids, but efforts to improve representation in bigger cities seem to be steps ahead of those efforts in Grand Rapids.

In late 2010, Sarah Scott, Tami VandenBerg, and I sat down to talk about planning an annual women's event in Grand Rapids. Sarah and Tami had planned a similar event in the past, and I had performed at a Ladyfest event in northern Michigan a few years prior. We decided to take on the Ladyfest name because of the solidarity it provided with events around the globe, but set off to do something distinctly local. Each year we tried to include new avenues to showcase the various talents, passions, and contributions of women. We had group bike rides and homebrewing workshops, discussions about how to negotiate pay, dance parties, panels on trans health, and everything in between.

The three of us had experienced working with local nonprofit organizations and agreed that the proceeds should benefit groups doing vital work on the ground that benefitted women. By focusing on this model, we hoped to illustrate the fundamental spirit of Ladyfest: women using their strengths to support other women, without the assistance of foundations or big-name funders.

We agreed that the methods in which the organizations served women would vary, but one thing had to be constant: beneficiaries had to be small enough that we knew the proceeds would make a big difference. Grand Rapids, while a small city, has a large number of women-serving nonprofits. There were obvious partnership options like the YWCA and Planned Parenthood, but we wanted to help fund organizations working at the grassroots.

Over the course of my five-year tenure on the planning committee, we donated to the Grand Rapids chapter of the National Organization for Women (NOW), Girls Rock! Grand Rapids, the Red Project's Sisters with Status peer group, and Our Kitchen Table. These groups felt like a good fit because we weren't aiming to land any large corporate sponsorships (although some fell into place anyway), but to organize our event in a way that small personal donations and admission costs would result in a moderate but heartfelt donation. We wanted to provide something tangible, whether that be instrument lessons for young girls in our community or the supplies to start a garden for a family struggling to make ends meet. Mostly we wanted to remind people how much community could get done through grassroots fundraising.

Over the years, the planning committee grew and changed, as did the challenges we faced. We were all volunteers. Many of us were parents, overworked in our respective careers, and going through intense personal life changes. Sometimes we dropped the ball. Thank you notes would be late. I would forget to update the website. We would fail to communicate important details to vendors. The reasons we sometimes dropped the ball were also the reasons we believed in LadyfestGR. It was a very human endeavor. We worked hard to make the event all-ages and accessible. We messed up a lot. We listened. We celebrated.

After five years, we agreed that operating with the same planning committee would be doing a disservice to the myriad of voices we tried to represent. Women ReVamped expressed an interest in taking over the event, and the committee decided that they could carry this on with the kind of intention and diversity it needed.

The void left by handing over the planning after so many years is real and I feel it every day. But the more that I step back from the work, the more I realize how beautifully feminine this whole process has been. We work so hard for what looks like little to nothing, and yet it feels so rewarding. Sometimes we put too much of our identity in that work. We rest when it's time. And all along the way, we take care of each other. I met some of my favorite people through this event, whether they attended, performed, presented, or met weekly in kitchens to talk about the budget, while our kids ran around screaming. I'm incredibly excited to participate in future Ladyfests as an attendee and to learn more about the power of this diverse community, knowing that it's going to keep growing to be better and better as it is shaped by new voices.

Unmasking Injustice

by Breannah Alexander

My time in Grand Rapids during the last two years has been interesting.

I have been angered beyond measure by the continued abuses of the Grand Rapids Police Department, and watching commentary from a police chief so empathy-deficient toward the trauma inflicted on black children that it makes me sick.

I have been given entry into spaces where folks are working hard to make positive systemic change in situations where the odds don't seem remotely in their favor.

I have met women of color working hard in a community that has a caste system that places them at the very bottom; victimized twice over by racial injustice and gender oppression.

Most importantly, I have met organizers, whose love exceeds understanding and explanation, continuously stand up in a space where they are the scapegoat for stagnation and the demon of choice in a community that has chosen to participate in palatable change at its convenience.

To be an organizer is the ultimate show of love for humanity—you have to give every single damn to do that work and do so unapologetically. I've seen individuals with that love put their commitment to social justice and equity (those are not the same thing by the way) before their own well-being. Organizers sacrifice so much to make communities better. In this community, organizers fall victim to misconceptions perpetuated by people who seek out power, influence, and prestige.

In Grand Rapids, to be an activist is to be a resident with a walking target on your back. In this community there is a fundamental misunderstanding around the nature of activism and the importance of cultivating and financially supporting those who elect to engage in such a strenuous line of work. This community is one that punishes expression when it doesn't fit the narrative developed by others (powerful, wealthy philanthropists), and brutalizes the oppressed into perpetual silence to ensure the interests of the powerful are executed at all times with no concern for the living collateral damage.

These are truths that residents will consistently confirm; with consequences that, for the activists who are left, result in their continued underemployment, and for some, a lack of access to the market at large. Another form of violence.

In Grand Rapids, the work to silence and oppress even happens in the places you least expect it: nonprofit organizations. Now one might ask how? The answer is simple: philanthropic dollars influence crucial decisions. Where a direct financial contribution to an individual may have gone against a series of legal ethical considerations, philanthropic dollars quietly (and not so quietly) influence policy making, employment decisions, and organizational management.

Angering the wrong influencers could mean the dissolution of an organization because there is an enormous amount of wealth held by the few in a community that desperately needs the investment. The subsequent results are a grant-seeking space where service providers bend to the wills of the financially influential and often ignore the real-time needs and desires of the communities they have expressly committed to serve. Sadly, the consequences are almost always the same: the most disenfranchised amongst us lose out whilst we, the nonprofiteers, boast about the success that numbers show we've had.

Little real progress is made.

So why does this matter? It's important to understand how the spaces we occupy function. It's important to note that Grand Rapids does not have a strong organizing community by design; if you have folks continually elevating injustice through direct action, protest, and organizing throughout the community, then it's harder to convince themselves and others of the utopian narrative that many Grand Rapidians have been socialized to believe.

In this community, it is vital for organizers to fight the narrative of perfection, as that is a tool for masking injustice. Much of my work centers around unmasking and creating spaces for honest dialogues to occur; that is where this community must begin before we can expect more radical action to happen in the context of change.

Contributors

Breannah Alexander is the Director of Strategic Programs at Partners for a Racism-Free Community. She is responsible for the management of all external community-based programming, education program design, and communications. Additionally, she is the founder and managing director of women re-Vamped, an organization established in response to a growing need for female-centered initiatives and a personal passion for ensuring the empowerment of young girls. Breannah's previous experience includes serving as the program manager of Michigan's Habitat for Humanity AmeriCorps Program, being an AmeriCorps state member at Grand Rapids Community Foundation, and six years working in various capacities with youth grantmakers in Michigan and across the nation.

Melissa Anderson is a lifelong volunteer. She promoted international understanding in high school, environmental quality while at Middlebury College in Vermont, reproductive choice when she worked in Washington, DC, and educational equity for women and girls as a member and president of the Grand Rapids branch of the American Association of University Women. She supported women running for office in her two terms on the Progressive Women's Alliance of West Michigan's board of directors, serving as chairperson from 2007 to 2010. After observing the growth in political influence of the religious right, Melissa became interested in supporting the religious left. She joined Plymouth United Church of Christ in Grand Rapids. Through Plymouth, Melissa has tutored an Iraqi refugee in English, lobbied state legislators for LGBTQ rights, testified before the state senate Energy & Technology Committee on solar power, attended monthly Black Lives Matter vigils, helped homeless families with the Interfaith Hospitality Network, and much more. Melissa is a retired business consultant. She and her husband, Mike Santoski, met in the MBA program at the University of Michigan in 1984, and have two children, Laura and David. They live in Cascade Township. While community activism is her idea of fun, Melissa's favorite hobby is reading.

Sara Badger is a Certified Professional Midwife and has been around birth for most of her life. Sara started her training as a teenager with her midwife mom, Anni McLaughlin. In 1999, Sara partnered with Anni and they worked together in Fresno, California, until 2007. She and her family moved to Michigan at the end of 2007. Sara started Simply Born Midwifery in 2010 and has been a gentle force of change in West Michigan's birthing community, promoting education and the expansion of services to ensure that women are empowered to make their own birthing choices. Sara has been married for fifteen years to Chris Howard and they have four children. She opened Cedar Tree Birth and Wellness Center, the first out-of-hospital birthing suite in West Michigan, in 2014, and opened Simply Born Birth House in October of 2016.

Elizabeth D. Barnum is Associate Minister of Education at Fountain Street Church in downtown Grand Rapids. Elizabeth is an ordained minister with standing in the United Church of Christ and is a graduate of Harvard Divinity School. Her passions include advocacy for comprehensive sexuality education across the lifespan. Writing, dancing, prayer, and being outdoors fuel her spiritual life and vocation.

Zyra Castillo teaches elementary through high school art in Grand Rapids. She has worked in the educational technology field, helping local and statewide schools with online curriculum, and writes lesson plans for her Art.Edukasyon blog. Zyra was born in Kawit, Cavite, Philippines. She spent most of her childhood in the Upper Peninsula before moving to attend Grand Valley State University for a bachelor's in Fine Arts and teaching certificate. She is an organizer of the Grand Rapids Asian Festival, has curated local shows for Avenue of the Arts's, Art.Downtown event since 2012. She is currently starting a Filipino pop up business, Gallafe, along with participating in other community groups.

Kelley Climie is currently pursuing a master's of social work at Western Michigan University. She lives in Grand Rapids, Michigan, with her husband Dan and their cats. Kelley would like to thank her parents, Maria and Darwin, her brother Joe, her family and friends, and the people of Grand Rapids. You are all worth fighting for.

Charlsie Dewey has spent most of her life in Grand Rapids. She is the digital editor for grmag.com and a freelance writer for the *Windy City Times* in Chicago. She spent five years as a reporter for the *Grand Rapids Business Journal*. Her activism began in 2009, when she attended her first Progressive Women's Alliance meeting at the Women's City Club—followed by drinks at the Cottage Bar. She was also a member of STOP WOW. In addition to pro-choice activism, she is involved in LGBTQ rights activism. She attended the University of Dayton in Ohio and spent a semester "abroad" at Chaminade University in Honolulu.

Reyna García is the owner of Reyna's Gallery Latino Cultural Art. She specializes in art that expresses deep passion, with a focus on causes of those under-represented, using art to represent the needs and the plight of Latinos and immigrants, both through the art itself and also through the forums through which her art allows her to speak and give voice to those causes. She has worked as a professional artist, self-employed for many years, and coordinator of the Mexican Cultural Project in New York City. As a cultural activist, she has contributed to the empowerment of women and community at large and has gained the respect and recognition from a number of local agencies and organizations as an advocate for the underprivileged. Her track record as an activist has been acknowledged by a number of organizations from New York to Chicago, particularly as a cultural activist on issues of social justice.

KT Herr is a transplant to Grand Rapids from Pennsylvania, by way of Massachusetts and Scotland. She holds a B.A. in English Language and Literature from Smith College, where she was a recipient of the Ruth Forbes Elliot Poetry Prize and the Rosemary Thomas Poetry Prize. She is the volunteer co-host of "Electric Poetry," a weekly poetry and interview show on 88.1 FM WYCE. Her work has been published in *Pilgrimage Literary Journal* and is forthcoming from the *3288 Review*. This year, she had the pleasure of being selected as a preliminary judge for the 2017 Dyer-Ives Poetry Competition. KT spent most of 2016 doing door-to-door fundraising for WGVU, Grand Rapids's public media member station, and subsequently transitioned into political canvassing throughout the fall on behalf of Michigan State Democrats. She was excited to helm the WGVU canvassing operation for the 2017 season as program director, but the dark specter of funding cuts eliminated the program at the eleventh hour. She's now back in the realm of the service industry, and changing hearts and minds one conversation at a time. However, she is relieved to be left with more time to devote to creative pursuits and is looking forward to volunteering with the Grand Rapids Pride Center in summer of 2017.

Jorja Jankowski started her career as an Outdoor Therapeutic Recreation Specialist. (outdoor recreation for people with disabilities). She organized and guided camping trips and other outdoor activities for people who have heard the word "can't" their whole life. She believes that everyone has the opportunity to discover his or her abilities in a positive, inclusive environment. Jorja was Outdoor Program Leader in Park City Utah, San Diego, California, and Carbondale, Illinois. Jorja is co-founder of Sixth Street Bridge Community Coalition. The coalition bridges the gap of available resources within the inner core of Grand Rapids. She began this venture by helping neighbors on the west side build and maintain community gardens and offering education on healthier alternatives within their diets. Jorja recently moved to Northern California and has already been involved with making a difference with neighborhood and community awareness, such as town walkability, increased access to community resources, and improvements on wheelchair-friendly access for businesses. Jorja has a bachelor's degree from Southern Illinois University in Therapeutic Recreation, and a master's of Social Work degree from Grand Valley State University.

José "Cha-Cha" Jimenez is one of seven founders of the Young Lords street gang and the founder of the Young Lords as a national human rights movement. He was born in Caguas, Puerto Rico, of Jíbaro parents on August 8,1948. He is in school and continues to lead the Young Lords in documenting their history for future generations. There have been several Lincoln Park Retreats at Yankee Springs and he currently is working on the Young Lords fiftieth anniversary celebration, to be held at DePaul University in Lincoln Park on September 21-23, 2018.

Michelle Jokisch Polo, a journalist and Grand Rapidian who originally hails from El Salvador and Ecuador, is bringing her expertise in advocating against systemic oppression, offering critical analysis, and listening to the community through her research to *Rapid Growth's* newest series, *On the Ground*. As the *On the Ground* editor, she will be spending much of her time over the next couple of months in the communities found along South Division Avenue that touch the Garfield Park and Burton Heights neighborhoods, learning from and listening to residents to celebrate this incredibly strong and diverse area through articles, photography, and more.

Mary Reed Kelly is a writer and business consultant who has collaborated in projects on diversity and cross-cultural communications, global curriculum development, and sales and negotiations skills for domestic and international corporations. As a resident of Grand Rapids for over twenty-five years, she's been an activist in the areas of anti-racism, public education, and health care policy. Mary received a B.A. in French Literature from Mount Holyoke College, and an M.B.A in Marketing and an M.A. in French Literature from the University of Kansas.

Jenny Kinne is a grassroots activist and nonprofit leader in Grand Rapids. She is currently working for the Michigan League for Public Policy as their community engagement specialist. In the past, Jenny worked for Planned Parenthood Advocates of Michigan, serving as West Michigan community organizer, where she built volunteer programming and community training initiatives to foster political activism. She also serves as the president of the local chapter of the National Organization for Women (NOW GR) and sits on the steering committee of the Fountain Street Church Choice Fund. Jenny grew up in Grand Rapids and moved back after college. She is passionate about policy advocacy, creating friendships across difference, and having conversations about the state of the world. Her favorite thing to do is curl up with her fur babies (two cats and a dog) with a good book.

Jeffrey D. Kleiman earned his doctorate in American History in 1985. After studying the role of religion and ethnicity in politics, he shifted his primary research field to the Holocaust and its aftermath, along with the role of memory and denial. Since 2002, Professor Kleiman has received two Fulbright awards for teaching in Poland along with archival research grants for work in Germany and Belgium. He has also been innovative in teaching approaches that include learning communities, interdisciplinary courses, study abroad, and distance education via compressed video, online, and blended formats. Dr. Kleiman's current project is completing a monograph on a Jewish survivor in Belgium, whose memoirs he has recently translated from Yiddish.

Jes Kramer is a musician and mama from Grand Rapids, Michigan. Her passions include all-ages music venues, radical parenting, feminism, fat acceptance, and LGBTQ rights. Kramer works as the business manager and assistant to the director at Wealthy Theatre, a historic theatre operated by Grand Rapids Community Media Center. She is one of the founders of LadyfestGR and served on the planning committee for five years. She's also an active volunteer with Girls Rock! Grand Rapids, serving as band coach and keyboard instructor. Aside from her job and activist work, Kramer strives to build progressive community through her music, which she has been writing and performing for over twelve years. She has released two EPs, two full-length albums, and is working on a third full-length currently. She also books shows and volunteers at the Division Avenue Arts Collective as a way to encourage increased access for youth, women, and queer folks in the West Michigan music scene.

Alex Markham has been a 93.9393 percent lifelong resident of Grand Rapids, with tenure spanning different school systems as a child and different neighborhoods as an adult. Holding a strong belief that you live where you serve, she is a proud resident of 49507. Alex is an active volunteer with Healthy Homes Coalition of West Michigan, Get the Lead Out, Michigan Alliance for Lead Safe Homes, Grand Rapids Homes for All, Kent County Habitat for Humanity, Team Rubicon, and All Hands Volunteers. Currently, she runs the peer education program through Healthy Homes Coalition of West Michigan. A lover of (almost) all things, in particular: her son Finn, books, volunteering, long rants along the beach, her grandmother's high heel collection, whiskey and ginger beer, intense talks with strangers, intense talks with pretty much anyone, her sister's love of holidays, getting lost but finding something else instead, voting, canvassing, dad jokes, her dad's jokes, strong loud-mouthed lady friends, singing Finn's name in Barry Manilow songs, hikes, goat cheese, her mother's ability to always remain the neutral Switzerland figure of the family, old mangy dogs, breezes, and the smell of dirt. She also wants to remind you: Vote in your local elections!

Julia M. Mason is an Associate Professor of Women, Gender, and Sexuality Studies at Grand Valley State University. She earned her doctorate in American Culture Studies, with graduate certificates in Women's Studies and Ethnic Studies, from Bowling Green State University, and a master of arts in American Indian Studies from the University of Arizona. Her community engagement and activism focus on gender justice, sustainability, and media literacy. She works to advance gender justice through teaching and service including coaching for *Girls on the Run* at Georgetown Elementary in 2015 and serving as the initial director of the GVSU Women's Leadership House.

Allison Manville Metz is an Associate Professor of Theatre Education and Theatre for Social Change at Grand Valley State University. "Dr. Alli" holds a Ph.D. in Theatre Research, and a B.A. in Theatre and English, from the University of Wisconsin-Madison, as well as an M.F.A. in Drama and Theatre for Youth from the University of Texas-Austin. Dr. Metz has led teacher-training workshops all over the United States and co-authored three editions of *Introduction to Integrating Music, Art, and Theatre* in Elementary Education, an arts integration textbook from Kendall Hunt Publishing. Dr. Metz is a proud, longtime member of the American Alliance for Theatre in Education (AATE), a national organization that named Metz the Winifred Ward Scholar in 2004. While teaching classes at GVSU, Alli also works with the GVSU Women's Center as the Director of ReACT!, a peer theatre education troupe which produces interactive theatre programming to help prevent incidents of violence against women on campus, a group that won a national AATE award in 2015. She is raising two socially-conscious daughters with her feminist husband in East Grand Rapids, Michigan.

John Nuerenberg was born in Detroit and raised in Edmore prior to attending Grand Rapids Community College (GRCC) and the University of Michigan. He joined the US Army, playing tuba in Army bands. Following three years in the Army, he attended Central Michigan University, graduating with bachelor's and master's degrees in music theory and composition. His professional career began in Grand Rapids, working at, and ultimately buying into, Christian Music Center, now known as Meyer Music. After nine years, he joined the staff at Yamaha Musical Products, working in several positions over twenty-two years as a product specialist, sales administrator, and IT specialist. When Yamaha closed in Grand Rapids, John found work in Arizona as IT manager in an architectural firm. John became very active in the national pro-choice movement, co-founding Pro-Choice Advocates of Greater Grand Rapids (PCA). He also founded the Coalition of Pro-Choice Organizations (COPCO), which helped to coordinate pro-choice activities in the city. He is still living in Arizona, but owns a cabin in the state of Washington, where he stays during the summer months. He is married (forty-eight years) to Sally, has two daughters, who both live in Washington, and two grandkids, ages nine and seven.

Ashley E. Nickels is an Assistant Professor of political science at Kent State University. Ashley is an interdisciplinary scholar whose primary field of study is public policy and administration, with emphases in nonprofit and community-based organizations, urban politics, and community organizing. She is the co-editor of *Feminist Pedagogy, Practice, and Activism: Improving Lives for Girls and Women* (Routledge, 2017). Though she was born and raised in Grand Rapids, she now lives in Shaker Heights, Ohio, with her amazing partner, awesome daughters, Tessa and Ella, and outrageous animals.

Mark Nickels was born in Grand Rapids and attended Godwin Heights Public Schools, then Catholic Central High School. He studied theatre at the University of Michigan, then returned to Grand Rapids to work at Schuler Books in its formative years. In 1994, he moved to New York, had a book of poems published, and was active in the poetry scene in Manhattan. In 2010 he moved to New England, and in 2015 received an M.S. degree in Counseling from the University of Massachusetts. He lives in Pelham, Massachusetts, and works as a mental health clinician in the nearby town of Ware.

Dia Penning is a connector of many disparate things. She supports deep conversation, reflection and action planning for sustained systems change. With a background in social justice, arts, education, and yoga, she makes space to imagine creative solutions to difficult problems. Dia has held positions at the San Francisco Arts Commission, California College of the Arts, Columbia College Chicago, and World Trust Educational Services. Currently she coordinates an intergenerational dialogue gathering at Commonweal in Bolinas, California. Dia has published three volumes of racial equity learning curriculum about systems and oppression, and is a seasoned facilitator and teacher. She runs an international program for Yoga and Social Justice, with Love Light Yoga, out of Vancouver, Canada, that focuses on the reimagining of colonialist legacies through cooperation, intentional liberation practices, and mindfulness. Founder of the Equity Collective, Dia seeks to embody honesty and nonviolence to support the deep investigation of social inequity. Through collaborating across discipline, she commits to the development of a society that embraces and supports all. Please contact her at dia@theequitycollective.com.

Marcel "Fable the Poet" Price is Poet Laureate of Grand Rapids Michigan. Author of *Adrift in a Sea of M&M's*, he is a biracial North American writer, teaching artist, community activist, and motivational speaker. Fable the Poet is highly-noted for his work with the youth, spreading mental health awareness using his own stories to consume the audience: "At times, we all feel fragile. We are paper boats entertaining the waves of life." He is an official partner of Mental Health America and is known across the nation for crowd-interactive features that leave those attending enlightened and empowered. Buckle up, prepare to make a new friend, and enjoy the ride.

Joel Potrykus is a filmmaker who has made three feature films (*Ape, Buzzard, The Alchemist Cookbook*), which have played SXSW, the Lincoln Center, AFI Fest, and overseas. Born and raised in Michigan, he continues to work with a small band of filmmakers, collectively known as Sob Noisse. He also teaches filmmaking at Michigan State University.

Bethany Reed is a mother. She is also the director of operations at Urban Pharm and a housing activist on the southeast side of Grand Rapids, Michigan. When she's not wrangling her two dogs, working on a home improvement project, or on a trip with her amazing teenager, you can usually find her at work, as she absolutely loves what she does for a living. Bethany holds a bachelor's degree in Communications and a real estate license and loves to volunteer her time (when she has it) to various housing, LGBTQ, and women's rights issues.

Lillian Reed lives in Grand Rapids, Michigan, and has her whole life. She is fifteen and has been volunteering at Planned Parenthood for several years and has long been involved in LGBTQ and reproductive rights activism. In her spare time, she draws and gardens. She goes to school at Grand River Prep.

Troy Reimink is a writer and musician living in Grand Rapids. His work has appeared in *Belt Magazine, the Detroit Free Press, the Grand Rapids Press, the Traverse City Record-Eagle* and several other regional publications. He also cohosts the *New Standards* community radio show every Sunday night on WYCE-FM (88.1).

Matthew Russell is a journalist and advocate for technology and equitable design in Grand Rapids, as well as a Midtown resident, currently living in the Old East End. His career experiences have spanned the fields of small town reporting, vegan baking and doughnut science, municipal landfill systems, cryptocurrency, and technical engineering.

Stelle Slootmaker, a fifth-generation Wyoming resident, began activism as a childbirth educator advocating for natural childbirth in the eighties with the Bloom Collective, STOK (Stop Targeting Our Kids), and as an *Indy News* contributor from 2005 to 2010. She has worked for food justice with Our Kitchen Table since 2010 and chairs the city of Wyoming's tree commission, the Tree Amigos, which she helped found in 2016.

Jeff Smith is a community organizer, writer, and director of the Grand Rapids People's History Project. For the past thirty-five years, Jeff has been involved in a variety of community-based organizing projects. From 1988-2006, Jeff worked in Guatemala, El Salvador, and Chiapas, Mexico, doing accompaniment work with organizations and communities receiving death threats from government security forces and death squads. Jeff founded the Grand Rapids Institute for Information Democracy (GRIID) in 1998. GRIID offers popular education classes, conducts media training, and produces independent journalism. Jeff has produced a documentary about his work in Central America entitled *Reversing the Missionary Position*. Jeff also wrote a book about his experiences in Latin America and working with refugees in Grand Rapids called *Sembramos, Comemos, Sembramos: Learning Solidarity on Mayan Time*. Jeff is currently working on a book called *A People's History of Grand Rapids*.

Marjorie Steele is a poet, writer, and citizen journalist and has been a resident of Grand Rapids for nearly ten years. A boomerang West Michigander, Marjorie has applied her writing background to marketing and communications in Grand Rapids's manufacturing and start-up sectors since 2008 and currently teaches business at Kendall College of Art and Design of FSU. Her writing can be found on Medium's subscription platform, *TheRapidian.org*, in Dyer-Ives's 2017 "Voices," and in various local publications.

Z. G. Tomaszewski, born in 1989 in Grand Rapids, Michigan, has two books of poems, *All Things Dusk* (International Poetry Prize winner selected by Li-Young Lee and published by Hong Kong University Press, 2015) and the chapbook *Mineral Whisper* (Finishing Line Press, 2017). Tomaszewski co-founded Great Lakes Commonwealth of Letters and has received fellowships from Beargrass Writing Retreat, Poets House of Montana, and the Moveen Prize (twice). Tomaszewski currently works maintenance at a 100-year-old Masonic Temple and is co-director of the Lamp Light Music Festival. New writing appears in *Blackbird, RHINO, the Cortland Review, diode,* and *Terrain.org,* among others.

Kathleen Underwood is associate professor, emeritus, of Women, Gender, and Sexuality Studies and History at Grand Valley State University, where she also served as chair of the Women, Gender, and Sexuality Studies Department. Kathleen traces her activism to her work in VISTA in the mid-1960s in rural North Carolina. Before earning her Ph.D. in American History, she was involved in the civil rights, anti-Vietnam War, and women's movements. Connecting on a personal level with students, she believes, has been a way to ensure that past social movements can provide examples and hope for change. Now retired, she is involved in social justice for immigrants and in electoral politics. She also spends time in her garden and reading mysteries in which the central characters are smart women.

Erika C. VanDyke has a master's degree from Michigan State University in Community Psychology and is passionate about the intersections in social justice, particularly as they relate to equity and public education. She has worked with Kent School Services Network, FoodCorps, the YMCA of Greater Grand Rapids, Kids' Food Basket, and LOOP at Sibley Elementary. She is an active member of the Latina Network of West Michigan and serves as the communications coordinator for the Latino Community Coalition. Erika was born in Bogotá, Colombia, and grew up in Grand Rapids. She returned to Bogotá recently to study Spanish, which she uses on a daily basis to advocate alongside students and families for resources and opportunities, and to build community both in the workplace and in the greater Grand Rapids area.

Dani Vilella is the Political and Advocacy Field Manager for Planned Parenthood of Michigan. She currently serves on the steering committee of the Fountain Street Church Choice Fund and the executive board of the Progressive Women's Alliance of West Michigan. She served five years as the president of the Grand Rapids chapter of the National Organization for Women, and three years as the vice president of action for the Michigan chapter. Dani is a graduate student at Grand Valley State University, earning her master's degree in Nonprofit & Public Administration. She holds a B.A. in Cultural Anthropology with a minor in Women and Gender Studies, also from Grand Valley State University, as well as a graduate certification in Nonprofit Leadership and Public Administration. She is a community organizer who is passionate about feminism, human rights, and sexual justice. Dani lives in Grand Rapids with her incredible partner, Jef, and their fabulous new baby girl, Madeleine.

Mindy Ysasi, leads the SOURCE. Their mission is to reduce employment barriers for employees that work for their partner organizations. Mindy joined the SOURCE in 2015 after an HR career in a variety of employment sectors, including healthcare and manufacturing. She is a graduate of Grand Valley State University with a B.B.A in management and marketing. Mindy is currently pursuing an EMBA at Michigan State University. In addition to be being one of the founding members of WorkLab Innovations—a network organization that is leading the replication and scale of the "sustainable workforce model," she is a co-founder of the Latina Network of West Michigan, an organic collective focused on changing the Latina narrative in the region. She is an appointed member to the Civil Service

Board, city of Grand Rapids, and she serves as the co-chair for KConnect (collective impact organization) high school to career work group. She has been recognized for her commitment and leadership with the Grand Rapids Area Chamber of Commerce ATHENA Young Professional award, the Grand Valley State University Alumni Service award, Grand Rapids Business Journal Forty under Forty, and the Young Nonprofit Professionals Network-Grand Rapids DoGooder and Exemplary Executive awards.

Acknowledgements

We want to thank all of the people who made this book possible. First, we want to start by thanking all of our financial supporters who donated through Kickstarter. We had 121 contributors, raising a total of $6,182.00.

Our sponsors for this book, individuals who gave $250 or more, include the following people:

Christie Cierlak and Bruce Lubben
Robert Goodrich
Brook Hayes
William (Rod) Lowe
Janis A. Lundquist
Ellyn Wolfson
Zachary D. Wood

We would also like to thank the contributors of this book, without whom we quite literally would not have a book. Thank you to Jenine Torres for her editing. Thank you to Jef McClimans for creating our Kickstarter video. And to Belt Publishing, thank you for believing in our idea and supporting us unconditionally along the way. While not Grand Rapidians, they know a thing or two about "grassroots." None of this would have been possible without the amazing people of Grand Rapids—the activists, the community organizers, residents, and the transplants. We are so grateful for all of the amazing people that live in and demand more from our city.

Dani:
To my family, Grama, Shawn, Tom, Gabe, Erin, Matt, Kylee, Thad, and Nathan (and their amazing partners), who support me in every crazy, ambitious project that I decide to undertake, giving money and time, showing interest, and celebrating my successes, thank you.

Thank you to my network of friends, colleagues, and fellow activists who stepped up, participated, and came through for me in contributing to this book.

To my beautiful baby daughter, Madeleine, this book is for you. You coming into my life reminded me how important my activism is and that it is my job to make the world a better place for you. I hope someday you will read this and be inspired to be an activist in your own right.

And, as always, thank you to my partner Jef. During the creation of this book I was pregnant, worked an intense election cycle, and gave birth. Throughout, he has been by my side, giving the time, the support, and the space that I needed to fulfill my dream of publishing a book. I could not have done it without him.

Ashley:
Thank you to my amazingly supportive family. To my brother, Connor, and his cool partner, Lisa, thank you for your unending support. I thank my extended family, who has given me so much over the years: money, places to stay, great stories, and so much love! Thank you to my partner, Aaron, and my daughters, Tessa and Ella. I love you all.

And, finally, to my mom and dad, who taught me to ask questions and challenge authority when that authority is being abused, this book is dedicated to you. You have shown me what it means to be brave and stand up for what I believe in; but more importantly you taught me the importance of listening to—and hearing—other people's stories.